PRAISE FOR *FROM THE CEO'S PERSPECTIVE*

"In a sea of too many leadership books, there are three reasons to read *From the CEO's Perspective*. First, author Teri Citterman is a phenomenal writer, and brings punch to the topic of leadership. Second, Teri lets a group of fantastic CEOs tell you their stories, so that you get direct insights from those who have been there and done that. Third, Teri brings her own unique experiences to the table, so that you get the additional perspective of a great writer, coach, and someone who is passionate about how we create more leaders in a world that needs them. I guarantee you that you will find at least one nugget of wisdom in this book that more than justifies your investment in reading it."

— Andrew Neitlich, Founder and Director,
Center for Executive Coaching

"Teri's writings on leadership are deeply inspiring and insightful. I was riveted to the comments of the leaders she interviewed for the book, and I took a lesson from each of them. Whether it be family influences or overcoming obstacles from their youth, to learning lessons by studying Abraham Lincoln, each had a story to tell and Teri has brought them to the world. This is an important study on leadership, and anyone would benefit by taking the time to read it."

— Kevin Glynn, Lighthouse Strategic Partners

"Teri went to the 'source' and tapped into the expectations and challenges of real business leaders. If you are trying to determine 'your fit' or 'your gaps' in the business leadership arena you will want to read this book!"

— Lindel James, CEO, Center for Leadership Skills

"The insight that Teri brings to the forefront of leadership challenges is critical for leaders of today to understand. Without the ability to measure ourselves as leaders from the perspective of how other successful leaders excel, we are robbing ourselves of an opportunity for greatness!"

— Skip Reynolds, master coach and certified trainer

"As I read the book, I was soaking in leadership lessons for my own personal development. Great read and packed with insights for leaders at all levels."

— Jag Randhawa, technology executive and award-winning author of *The Bright Idea Box*

"If you want to be a relevant leader who is on the winning side of progress, you'll be thankful you read this book."

— Michael Fulmore, author of *Unleashing Your Ambition*

"To succeed you need to study success! Teri has done this by capturing an inside perspective from some of the most successful CEOs and greatest leadership minds. When you apply this knowledge to your own leadership, life and career, you will soar to new heights and achieve your destiny!"

— Patrick Snow, international best-selling author of *Creating Your Own Destiny* and *The Affluent Entrepreneur*

"Teri has developed an extremely valuable roadmap that gives the reader an insider's view of how 20 high profile CEO's define, measure and develop leaders in their companies. Having access to this information coupled with personal insight gained from answering several self-reflective questions Teri poses at the end of each chapter will fast-track your quest to become a better leader while simultaneously learning how to instill this capacity in others. Buy this book, read it and profit from the inner-wisdom you will gain by going through this journey!"

— Earl Bell, Principal and Founder, EarlBell.com, Author, *Winning in Baseball and Business*

"If you want to get a fresh perspective of what it takes to be a difference maker in today's volatile and constantly changing business environment, you will benefit from and enjoy reading this well researched book by Teri Citterman."

— Otto Stimakovits, principal, CBO

"As a former executive in the automotive industry, all I can say is WOW! Teri is bang on with her approach and has done her research. If you want to succeed in the boardroom or in life you have to get this book!"

— Nicole Gabriel, author of *Finding Your Inner Truth*

FROM THE CEO'S PERSPECTIVE

LEADERSHIP IN THEIR OWN WORDS

TERI CITTERMAN

From the CEO's Perspective:
Leadership in Their Own Words

Published by Aviva Publishing
Lake Placid, NY
518-523-1320
www.avivapubs.com

ISBN: 978-1-940984-27-8

Library of Congress Control Number: 2014908464

Editor: Allan Halcrow
Cover & Interior Design: Fusion Creative Works, fusioncw.com

Every attempt has been made to properly source all quotes and attribute all research.

Printed in the United States of America.

First Edition

For additional copies visit:
FromtheCEOsPerspective.com
TalonnLLC.com

Also available in e-book

DEDICATION

To Pradeep Rajurs

When another person believes in you 1000%, that's potent. That support, that love, that empathy offers a steady stream of motivation. Raj, you have no idea how you've inspired me; but I do.

To My Mom and Dad

Separately, Ruth and Klaus Citterman survived a tragic time in the world's history. And while neither of them had much in the way of a childhood, they provided an empty canvas and a rich story for me to make my own.

A MESSAGE TO READERS

To CEOs and those who
aspire to be a CEO,
join the conversation at
#CEOpov

ACKNOWLEDGEMENTS

First of all, I should acknowledge that I don't think I can get discounted tickets on Alaska Airlines; but thank you, Brad Tilden. I *can,* however, get free checking at JP Morgan Chase, but I don't think that's special for me. Nonetheless, thank you, Phyllis Campbell.

And thank you to all the leaders who were generous with their time, willing to respond to my emails and agreeable to meeting my deadlines. What an absolute honor and privilege it is to know all of you.

Thank you Allan Halcrow, my editor and friend. It's like the *Thelma and Louise* road trip we've been on is ending, so we need to either drive off the cliff or write another book. I'm not sure which is more compelling. Because I have a bit of an attitude when it comes to writing, my expectations were low. But Allan threw down the first three sentences (you know the ones) and blew my mind! I've never been the same since. Thank you for being such a fun and amazing partner on this journey.

Thank you to my mentor and dear friend Mike Kunath. From the start, Mike believed in me far more than I believed in myself. I listened and learned and over time that changed. The lessons could be annoying and the debates could be fierce. It's the cribbage games that always brought us back to center. Mike told me I could make a difference, and I will not disappoint him.

Mike Flynn, thank you for always being one of my biggest fans and promoters. Thank you to those who connected and supported me: Sunrise Swanson (whom I met on LinkedIn), Nancy Cho, John Meisenbach, Shelley Tomberg, Stacy Lill, Matan and Sinclair, Stan Herring, Herb Bridge, Jamie Peha, Sandy Sharma, Marty Curry, Cynthia Ely, Jason Stoffer, Jan Gelman, Amanda Weber Welch, Madelyn Welch, Shiv Rajurs and Maya Welch. Thank you Patrick Snow, and your awesome team of talent.

It takes a village!

CONTENTS

INTRODUCTION:
TWO BEGINNINGS

My passion for leadership – a passion that shaped my career and ultimately led to writing this book – has two beginnings: One in 1938 Germany, and the other a serendipitous introduction to a man at the Four Seasons Hotel in Seattle 62 years later. These beginnings – seemingly unrelated – are, in fact, deeply connected. Each represents an essential half of any effective leadership: First, the wish to lead and, second, the learned skills to do so.

First, to Germany and my development as a Survivor Archetype. My parents were Holocaust survivors. And while this is not *that* story, it does explain my innate leadership. My dad, Klaus Citterman (1921-2009), escaped Germany in 1938. That same year, at the age of 10, my mom, Ruth Levinson Citterman, fled Austria with her parents. (Incidentally, my mom, at 86, still lives independently in Portland, Oregon, where they met.)

Where does the Survivor Archetype come from? On November 9, 1938, in Germany and parts of Austria, the Nazis orchestrated a series of coordinated attacks against Jews. The attacks became known as Kristallnacht (the night of broken glass), and the morning after them my dad, just 17 years old, was arrested and taken to the city's central train station. There, he was lined up for deportation to Buchenwald concentration camp. Instead of accepting this destiny, something in him tempted fate.

He approached a Nazi soldier and requested he be released. (This is the 140-character version.) He pled his case, and was taken – his heart pounding – to hide in empty rooms, behind open doors. By the end of the day, he was released. The Nazi soldier escorted him out through the gates of the station and gave him bus fare to get home.

By that point, all the world's doors had closed to Jews. But a desperate appeal yielded three tickets to China, the only land that didn't require a visa for entrance. My dad and his parents escaped to Shanghai, where the culture and language couldn't have been more different. He survived there for nine years, working in various mechanical jobs and learning the automotive trade, before coming to the United States in 1947.

Although my parents found their own personal strength in tragic and traumatic circumstances, I absorbed the Survivor Archetype from them as I grew up. This archetype is described as having the ability to thrive on struggle; I would include the ability to embrace ambiguity. Survivors find the sense of security stagnant and stifling. Hence, Survivors often seek risk rather than contentment.

The Survivor Archetype is alive and well in me – flowing through my veins, constantly penetrating my psyche. And yes, there's an obvious question. How is it that someone born in 1970 has parents who experienced Holocaust atrocities firsthand? At the time of my birth, my mom was 42 and my dad, 50. These would-be trendsetters were among the pioneering parents of the "later-in-life" baby phenomenon, which today is recognized as normal. That's how it happened. And, given that I wasn't my parents' first rodeo, I joined an already-made family of two older sisters and an older brother. They had a head start of 13 to 19 years, and their formative years took place in a time of unprecedented social change. One could say I was the beneficiary of their fresh thinking.

My oldest sister had the greatest impact on me. Her teen years, during the 1960s and '70s, were shaped by the disorder and chaos of the counterculture thinking of the times. The upshot is that she gave me the message of equality and challenged the traditional roles of women. She instilled in me that I could be anything I wanted to be, and I believed her.

She said I could run faster than the boys, so I beat them every chance I could. She said I could be a homerun hitter, so every time I stepped up to the plate (on my mixed boys and girls baseball team), I hit the ball harder and farther than anyone else. At nine years old, it was pretty satisfying to hear the coach of the other team tell his outfielders to back up "because that *girl* is up to bat again."

In the earliest stages of my life, my sister inspired my self-confidence and an aggressive, no-fear conviction. While I've worked hard to temper the aggressiveness, that sense of self and risk-taking continues to shape me today. (Yes, trapeze is a hobby of mine.)

LEARNED LEADERSHIP

Given my background, I suppose it's no surprise that throughout my life, I've been borderline obsessive in my need to understand the complicated issues related to authority – leadership, power and influence. But I still had to learn leadership skills. That's why we move forward to a fortuitous introduction at the Four Seasons Hotel in Seattle. That's when I met a man who became my mentor and remains a close friend and ally.

On October 31, 2000, I was looking for a job. I had a job in a large mobile phone company, but it was the dot com era, and I was curious about what was going on beyond the walls of traditional corporate America. Job hunting and interviewing was sort of a hobby for me. Looking back, I think it was a strategic way of networking.

In the process, I connected with a man who has since passed away, but was known as a pillar in our community. Dick Friel suggested I take my resume to the Four Seasons Hotel (now the Fairmont) around 4 p.m. that afternoon. He told me to look for the man in an Italian suit with a corn-cob pipe: "His name is Michael."

That afternoon, I spotted the man sitting at a table in the bar. I approached him cautiously, and he invited me to join him and a few others for a drink. I handed him my resume. He glanced at it, asked a few questions and then his phone rang.

While he turned away to take the call, the woman sitting across from me struck up a conversation. She lamented about how difficult it was to select the right boarding school for her daughter. I wasn't really qualified to weigh in, so I just listened. The man next to her mentioned that he had a suit of armor collection, 14 of which he had just sold to buy a castle somewhere in Europe.

Who are these people?

Mike hung up his phone and turned back to me. "You do PR, right?"

I nodded.

"How would you deal with a reporter in regards to a very high-profile commercial real estate deal?" His tone was curt and commanding. He told me the details of a deal he was involved in and insisted this information was highly confidential. He insinuated that if the deal went through, perhaps I'd have a job handling the PR.

I knew this was a test and started to formulate a smart response, but before I had an opportunity to respond, a reporter from the *Seattle Times* walked up. He joined us at the table and introduced himself. He was new to the commercial real estate beat and wanted to pick Mike's brain.

Mike began to tell the reporter the same information he had told me "in confidence."

The reporter reached for a pad and pen, and Mike waived it away. He leaned in. "No names, everything on background – off the record. If you fuck me, I'll never work with your paper again. Understand?" The table was quiet; the reporter nodded. Mike proceeded. I knew this wasn't his first press encounter, but I sat beside him and cringed.

When he finished, he turned to me. "I can see by your body language, you would have handled this information differently. What would you have said?"

I froze. I was a deer in the headlights in an incredibly awkward, three-way with a reporter. I began to tell Mike what I would have done differently, and he interrupted. "Am I being lectured?" he demanded.

"Perhaps," I responded.

Mike abruptly ended the conversation, and the three of us exchanged business cards. The reporter and I exchanged "WTF" glances and he left the table.

Mike turned to me again. "Well, what are you going to do for dinner?" he demanded in his low voice.

Is this guy hitting on me?

"Listen," he said. "I'll take you to dinner on the condition I can ask you 30 minutes of questions."

I was curious. I said, 'I'll go to dinner with you on the condition I can ask *you* 30 minutes of questions."

He agreed. We drove in his car to Il Terrazzo Carmine. When we arrived, Mike's table in the corner of the bar was set, "his" bottle of Italian white wine already chilling. As we sat down, Mike spoke rapidly. "I'm married with three kids. My oldest daughter is probably your age. This isn't about what you're thinking. I believe you have the ability to make a difference." Silence.

He quickly moved to his next topic. "Name the top five things you want in your next job; three words or less."

I named them. We prioritized them. The night went on. "If I could be anything," I told him, "I'd want to be a travel writer."

"Hmmm. Not what I heard at the hotel."

At the end of the evening, he invited me back to the Four Seasons the following Tuesday to meet some "people you should know. If you come to 10 of these, you'll have 10 different job offers," he said.

He sent me home with a driver. When I woke up the next day, I had no idea how life was about to change.

The next Tuesday, when I arrived at the Four Seasons, 10 businessmen were gathered around a table full of cocktails. Mike led the three-ring circus and demanded that everyone around the table introduce themselves and explain why they were there. Everyone introduced himself, and then broke off into side conversations. This would become a familiar ritual for me.

After two hours or so of this type of session, we would leave. Mike would take me to dinner and drill me for 20 minutes. "What was the dynamic between player A and player B? What did you see in the body language of player C? Who was the weakest link at the table and who had the most power?" The fire hose of questions went on and on.

During these sessions, I learned to listen closely, process information quickly, assess the dynamics of the people and understand the subtleties of the situation. I practiced as a devoted student. I stopped looking for a job and started my own public relations business. I honed my strategic thinking skills and developed my interpersonal skills; both, research tells us, are lacking in today's leaders.

Through this sometimes informal, but usually formal, mentorship the experience was profound. It made me deliberate in how and what I thought, how I supported my thinking, and how I acted. I began to perceive the world through the measurement of influence, and internalized the mantra that "power is always in the question."

Today, I've chosen a career (or perhaps it's chosen me) centered on high potential, mid-level managers who are on the trajectory to the top. So naturally, a blog post on leadership in *The Huffington Post* caught my eye. Here we are living in a time of great opportunity. Technology offers global access at an unprecedented level. And yet, as a country we are not positioned to fully absorb or exploit these opportunities. According to research cited in the article (not to mention word on the street and almost any new business book you read), the demand for leadership talent significantly exceeds supply. *The Huffington Post* piece cites research by AON Consulting showing nearly 60% of U.S. companies face leadership talent shortages.

We talk about the gap between the haves and the have-nots, about the gap in achievement, about the earnings gap. Why aren't we talking more about the gap in leadership?

SO I STARTED ASKING

The blog post piqued my interest so much that I started asking:

What are leaders in our community doing to develop future leaders?

I talked to a few friends who are CEOs of higher-profile companies. I wanted to know what characteristics they look for in emerging leaders. Do they have an unspoken list in their head of who those up-and-comers are? And how do they, personally, interact with those they see as the next leaders in their organizations?

And that led to asking a few others, which led to additional questions and additional conversations. I asked, "Who had a great impact on your leadership?" and "What famous leaders do you most admire or identify with?"

Since no two CEOs are alike, and there are rarely forums in which to hear such views, I thought others might find value in hearing these conversations. Thus, the idea for this book emerged. At that point, my goal was to include a few CEOs from a few different industries. In the end, I was privileged to speak with 20 leaders from a myriad of sectors, for-profit and non-profit organizations. CEOs from companies such as Alaska Airlines and KING 5 agreed. CEOs and presidents of non-profits like Special Olympics and Seattle Foundation agreed. And the chairman of a hybrid company like Oki Developments, which houses for-profit and non-profits under one roof, said yes.

Much of the discussions that followed reinforced what recent research on leadership tells us. But just as often, the leaders expressed their opinions, observations and judgments. Both sides of the discussions inform the leadership lessons in this book – and so does one other important factor. How we see leadership – how we believe we should lead and how we want to be led – is very different from one generation to another. Maybe it isn't surprising that each generation sees the others in largely unflattering ways. But understanding those differences – the truths and the myths – is crucial to whether we can successfully develop leaders for the future.

WHAT'S NEXT?

Understand, this book is a roadmap – a collection of personal experience and insight on how leaders develop leaders.

You'll learn several perspectives on defining and measuring leadership, and what each CEO looks for in emerging leaders. You'll learn how they develop leaders what they do personally, what they see as the biggest challenges facing up-and-coming leaders, their one "must-have" trait and their advice.

These conversations were personal and intimate, and the learning was invaluable. I think you'll agree.

Use this book to challenge your thinking on how you define your own leadership and how you serve to develop others. This book is written for new CEOs who are striving to make a mark on the changing landscape of leadership. It's for the up-and-comers, the high performers who are pursuing executive roles. And it's for seasoned CEOs who have a genuine curiosity about how other leaders think and approach leadership.

As you read about leadership in *their* words, I challenge you to get clear on your own leadership and put it into *your* own words. The end of each chapter includes a handful of questions, about who impacted you as a leader, your role as a mentor, how you view generational stereotypes, your core values, how you identify leaders, your greatest leadership strength, your 'must-have' traits and what you see as significant derailers. You get the gist.

This is your chance to focus your thoughts while they're top of mind. Then, at the end of the book, you'll be more aware of who you are as a leader and how you relate to your own strengths and values. With that knowledge, you can't help but be a more thoughtful, deliberate and effective leader.

At that point, step into action. Get clear on whom you want to develop and set the ball in motion. The work requires passion, commitment and time, and your impact will be significant.

Write in ink. Good luck!

THE LEADERS

1. Alaska Airlines, **Brad Tilden**, CEO
2. Apptio, **Sunny Gupta**, CEO
3. Ben Bridge Jeweler, **Jonathan (Jon) Bridge**, Co-CEO & General Counsel
4. Columbia Hospitality, **John Oppenheimer**, CEO
5. Gravity Payments, **Dan Price**, CEO
6. GreenRubino, **John Rubino**, Partner
7. International Community Health Services, **Teresita Batayola**, CEO
8. JP Morgan Chase (Pacific Northwest Region), **Phyllis Campbell**, Chairman
9. Maveron, **Dan Levitan**, Co-Founder & Managing Partner
10. NBC KING 5, **Ray Heacox**, President & General Manager
11. Oki Developments, **Scott Oki**, Chairman
12. Project Bionic, **Josh Dirks**, Co-Founder & CEO
13. Seattle Foundation, **Norm Rice**, CEO & President
14. Seattle Metropolitan Chamber of Commerce, **Maud Daudon**, CEO
15. Seattle University, **Father Stephen Sundborg**, President
16. Special Olympics of Washington, **Beth Wojick**, CEO
17. Ste. Michelle Wine Estates, **Ted Baseler**, CEO
18. Tom Douglas Restaurants, **Pamela Hinckley**, CEO
19. University of Washington Medicine, **Dr. Paul Ramsey**, CEO
20. Xtreme Consulting, **Greg Rankich**, CEO

PART 1: FROM THEIR PERSPECTIVE: THEIR STORIES, THEIR PASSION

NO-BOUNDARIES DNA

It seems entirely right that I first met Mike – and deepened my passion for leadership – in Seattle. Not Dallas, not San Francisco, not even New York or L.A. Seattle. And throughout my many conversations with Mike, there's been no shortage of pontification on what makes this area unique. The city – and the surrounding Puget Sound region – is unequivocally one of few urban landscapes on Earth with an earned reputation for propagating best-of-breed companies. They innovate and achieve at the highest levels, and ultimately dominate their respective industries.

It started in the early part of the 20th century with the rise of raw-materials manufacturer Weyerhauser, now one of the world's largest private owners of timberlands. Paccar (the third-largest manufacturer of medium and heavy-duty trucks) and Boeing (one of the world's largest commercial aircraft manufacturers) soon followed. Each capitalized on opportunity and entrepreneurship and went on to become the dominant player in its industry.

The second half of the century birthed such companies as upscale fashion retailer Nordstrom and technology giant Microsoft. Hundreds of companies later spun out of Microsoft, including the online travel company Expedia, which achieved the same ambition of best-in-breed status barely 20 years later. Costco launched and quickly became the second-largest US retailer. Starbucks opened its doors and is now the largest coffeehouse company in the world. And then there's Amazon, now the world's largest online retailer.

Microsoft and Amazon rank as the third and fourth most successful start ups of all time, book-ended by a couple of no-name Bay Area companies. OK, I'm competitive. Unless you live on a different planet, you know their names, but that's not the point.

The point is that people who come to the greater Seattle area have an extreme desire to be successful. And there's a high probability of meeting others with that same aspiration. Either they've been successful or they anticipate success and, most important, they refuse to be left behind. Remember, barely 100 years ago Seattle truly was the Wild West. People were gun-totin' outlaws who had a "You can!" mentality and a "Go to hell" message for non-believers. One might conclude not much has changed.

But what else?

What is it about the Puget Sound region that legitimizes the claims of business dominance across multiple industries? It could be that the weather actually *is* an advantage; it's easy to maintain laser focus when it's dark and rainy most days of the year. Or, it could be that our water has literally turned to coffee. We're jacked up, and we've found a positive way to channel our obsessive-compulsive behaviors into excessive productivity.

It could also be our Midwestern heritage, with a strong foundation of values firmly rooted in hard work, individualism and determination. Or it could be because we're a saltwater community that looks east for the past, and west for the future.

Whichever way you choose to see it, you can attribute the Puget Sound's powerful culture for nurturing dominant innovation to five characteristics. Companies here:

1. Are lead by strong individual entrepreneurs
2. Create a new business niche
3. Become dominant in that niche
4. Remain independent
5. Maintain a heavy emphasis on customer service

Certainly, those characteristics are true of the company leaders I've interviewed. Their words are steeped in this culture; their styles and perceptions align with the no-boundaries DNA of the Puget Sound.

ORIGINS OF PASSION

But they also can trace their own passions for leadership to different sources, and find inspiration in different role models. You know now where my passion comes from; let's look at the origins of theirs. Who had a key impact on their leadership? And of all the famous leaders they know or have read about, who does each CEO most identify with?

ALASKA AIRLINES
BRAD TILDEN, CEO

POWER IS STRONG AND GENTLE

My dad contracted polio when he was 19 years old. He went through life without the use of one leg, and his other leg was pretty darn weak. But he didn't let that stop him. He persevered, and that helped shape me as a leader. He chose to have a bright outlook on life, went to school, and earned two engineering degrees. He and my mom raised six kids, he worked at Boeing, and they built a really great life. I never heard him complain about his situation. In fact, I only remember him talking about his polio a couple of times. He was a powerful example of someone who was very strong, who had really high standards, yet was very gentle.

I identify with Abe Lincoln for similar reasons. During the Civil War, things were chaotic in our country. Lincoln's cabinet members had all competed for his job and there was a lot of dissension, but he was gentle and quiet and gave people room to be themselves. At the right time, he brought people together, provided great leadership, and ended slavery.

APPTIO
SUNNY GUPTA, CEO

THE BEST ARGUMENT WINS

My approach to leadership started with my parents. A core practice I learned in my family was debate. My parents didn't necessarily expect us to have the winning argument. But they did expect us to hone our thinking and to make the strongest argument possible. I use those skills today, and it's something I'm trying to teach my children.

My father, in particular, also taught me to be fair always. When he had to resolve family issues, he was very fair with everyone. Lastly, staying humble is another important principle I learned. I didn't grow up privileged. I think when you come from a humble background, you have a greater desire to succeed. Maybe it's the idea of having a chip on your shoulder; maybe you're hungrier. But it causes people to be driven. You can see it in this country in the story of immigrants. And you can see it in some of the great NFL players who succeeded despite their circumstances and continue to stay humble.

I thought it was great to see Satya Nadella become CEO of Microsoft, because every time I've met him I think, 'Boy, he's a humble guy. He's really trying to learn the market and about the customers.' When we met, he was so interested in what was happening here at Apptio, and genuinely wanted to learn and understand. Continuous learning and improvement is what separates the great leaders from the good ones.

Others who have had a key impact on me are my board members Tom Bogan, from Greylock Partners, and Yuval Scarlat, a former senior vice president of products at Mercury Interactive. Tom helped me hone general leadership principles, such as how to build a culture and how to develop talent – those types of things. Yuval helped me really understand the glass-half-empty approach, meaning he helped me see the value of focusing on the things that aren't working. He also taught me to always keep the customer's perspective front and center. If you do those things, other things fall into place.

I admire how Jeff Bezos, founder and CEO of Amazon, and the late Steve Jobs, co-founder, chairman and CEO of Apple, were able to innovate from within. Big companies usually have a hard time innovating. But Amazon went from a book e-tailer to a Web retailer to selling groceries to offering Web services to creating the Kindle. Bezos has been able to innovate at scale in a systematic way, and I think that's a result of his leadership principles.

With Apple, Jobs was able to resurrect the company and transform it into one of the most innovative companies on the planet. It's ironic because here in Seattle we see it as Apple versus Microsoft, and who would have thought everyone would be using an iPhone? When I read Job's biography, I recognized his leadership principles were very different from mine, but it's still amazing that he was able to do what he did and the company was able to succeed as it has.

BEN BRIDGE JEWELER
JON BRIDGE, CO-CEO & GENERAL COUNSEL

EVERYONE IS MOST IMPORTANT

My parents had the biggest influence on my leadership. With my dad, it goes back to the Navy, and caring about people and treating each person as if he is the most important person in the room. He taught me to pay attention and to make the person you're with feel important. It may be that you can't wait until the meeting is over, but you don't ever show that. My dad exudes radiance, and that's a big reason why he achieved the rank of admiral in the Navy. With my dad, everyone is a 'good friend.' My mom was different. She formed very deep connections with people. My mother exhibited empathy and made a personal difference in people's lives. I have a lot of both of them in me, but I don't do it as well as they did.

A lot of what I value in leadership draws on my Jewish roots. *Tikkun olam* is a Hebrew phrase that means, 'repairing or healing the world'. There are so many people I admire for what they've contributed to healing the world. I admire Warren Buffet for the philanthropic choices he's made to make the world a better place. I admire people who sacrifice time or money or a combination. I admire Bill Gates and, even more so, his father and mother. And Melinda Gates is doing fantastic things for the world. I admire my wife, Bobbe, for establishing the Center for Children and Youth Justice and carrying out its focus on systemic change in juvenile justice and child welfare systems. To me, that is true leadership.

COLUMBIA HOSPITALITY
JOHN OPPENHEIMER, CEO

TREAT THE PRISONERS WELL

My family had the greatest impact on my life. I think most successful people could make that claim. Even so, at the risk of sounding mundane, my parents and grandparents deserve a lot of credit.

My dad was a successful entrepreneur. I watched him build successful businesses, which he did by treating everyone nicely, no matter his or her status. It didn't matter if it was his most important client or someone struggling on the street. He consistently treated everyone like royalty, as if each person was the most important person in the world. He learned this principle from my grandfather, his father-in-law, Leo Falk.

My mom's family lived down the street from the Idaho state prison. Anyone who wanted to date my mom (Leo's youngest daughter) had to meet with Leo first. He'd take the prospective date on a walk down the road to the jail. They'd enter the stone-cold facility, pass by the guards, and walk the rows of cells. Leo would greet each prisoner. He'd judge my mother's potential suitor's character based on how he treated the prisoners. Few of the courters passed the test – but I guess my dad was the exception. Not only did he pass, he went on to instill in all of us the value of always treating people with dignity and respect.

When I was 12, my dad took me with him on his business trips. He sold food products, and I got to watch him in action. My dad had a great passion for meeting and embracing people. It was the way he learned from them, and this was his way of spending time with me and teaching me how to understand people.

My parents were lifelong learners. At 60 years old, my mom learned Spanish. Very late in life, my dad decided to change religions and learned the Bible from a whole new perspective. Learning and doing and living with enthusiasm is what kept them young and lively. One of the core values of our company, and the one I value most, is enthusiasm. In my opinion, to have a strong sense of adventure and willingness to learn – and to approach life with enthusiasm – creates a perfect storm for success.

GRAVITY PAYMENTS
DAN PRICE, CEO

BE THE HEAVIEST STRAW

Abraham Lincoln was a huge influence on me as a leader. I appreciate that he was willing to do or say whatever it took to accomplish his goal – even if it violated other parts of his value system. He was really focused on one thing and getting that one thing done. There aren't too many things in life that are so important that it doesn't matter what you do to accomplish them.

At the same time, he maintained humor and understated his place in life. He was the straw that broke the camel's back – he knew he wasn't everything on the camel. He just knew he had to be the absolute heaviest straw possible or the back wasn't going to break. That was amazing, because we know how much he valued honesty – and he was willing to lie, cheat and steal to serve a greater good.

When I was a kid, my parents read *Les Miserables* to me and I've been inspired by the story of Jean Valjean. He's another person for whom there were rules and values and principles. Are you going to pay greatest attention to the rules? Or to the 'why' behind the rules and how they sit with your values? You have to be so committed to your values. Values have to be the number one thing that people can trust you on – not what you're doing, not how you're doing it, but *why* you're doing it. Valjean exemplifies that to me. He faced adversity head on and was willing to take risks. He was committed to changing the things he saw his family going through, so that fewer families would have to endure such hardship.

GREENRUBINO
JOHN RUBINO, PARTNER

YOU CAN DO MORE THAN YOU THINK YOU CAN

When I worked for Landor Associates in New York, an executive, Peter Harleman, opened himself up to being my mentor. It was the right time in my career, and I recognized the value of that type of learning. Pete advised me and served as a personal sounding board for all my questions and ideas. When a position a few rungs higher than mine became available, Pete provided advice and support, and worked behind the scenes to help me get that position. Pete created a win-win, where I learned from a real leader. One of the biggest lessons I learned from Pete is that you can do more than you think you can. Pete helped me recognize my own strengths, but in order to achieve at a higher level I had to sell myself to myself. I needed to convince myself that I could do the job, and I did. I don't think I've ever sold myself short since.

Courage is the difference between a good leader and a great one. Courage is multi-faceted, an overarching theme that encompasses a lot of ideas. You have to have the courage to be honest and take risks. By that, I mean the courage to take risks when no one is watching – to do it because it's right, not because you want the credit. To do something courageous when no one is watching is pretty cool. It takes courage to make decisions – especially the tough ones. It takes courage to trust and listen and delegate. It takes courage to take responsibility when things go wrong. I hang my hat on courage.

INTERNATIONAL COMMUNITY HEALTH SERVICES
TERESITA BATAYOLA, CEO

BE THE POWER BEHIND THE SCENES

I'm an immigrant, so there was a lot of transition in my life. I've tended to 'collect' people over the years. I can think of many who had an impact, from the nun who was my school principal – who told me I was not trying hard enough – to someone like Ruth Woo, famous in our community as a power behind the scenes. Ruth is a selfless community leader whose influence rests on mentoring countless people who have achieved powerful positions, especially in elected office. She has mentored Gary Locke (US ambassador to China and former Washington state governor), Ron Sims (former deputy secretary of the United States Department of Housing and Urban Development and former King County executive), and Jennifer Belcher (Washington secretary of state), among others. Professionally, she was an administrative assistant to leaders like former Governor Dan Evans and to Lands Commissioner Brian Boyle. She wielded her influence to open doors and champion many causes, always working behind the scenes to bring the right people together. Ruth is a model for the ability to influence without using the hammer of a title. She talked directly to decision makers or used the power of her network to get to decision makers.

Another person who strongly influenced me was Merritt Long, whom I knew when I worked for the State Commission for Vocational Education. I was young, probably thought of as a high performer. Merritt was in awe of my energy level. He was quiet, and reflective, with a sense of impish humor whenever we talked. I was probably thought of as a little too opinionated. He helped me ground my ideas by questioning me: 'TB, have you thought about this or that or taken different people's opinions and influence into account?' Then he would say, 'Hey, you want to do the work? Go for it!'

JP MORGAN CHASE
PHYLLIS CAMPBELL,
CHAIRMAN, PACIFIC NW REGION

GET READY!

Gerry Cameron, who's now retired, coined the term 'Get Ready.' Gerry was one of my early business mentors, my first boss at US Bank. He always said, 'Phyllis, get ready!'

And I'd say, 'Get ready for what?'

He was referring to me as a woman in banking. He knew how women struggled, especially in this industry. He said, 'For someone like you, you always have to be in a mental state of readiness. You must be at the top of your game, because when that door opens, you have to be really ready to walk through it.' He knew sometimes women had lower levels of confidence and a diminished sense of value, and he wanted to make sure I would be ready.

Eventually, we were having a conversation about my career future. He asked me what I wanted to do. I said, 'How about I take your job?' Gerry was president of US Bank of Washington. A few weeks later, he called and offered me his job. I tried to back out by saying I wasn't ready – that I didn't think I was good enough. He dismissed it all and just said, 'Move on Phyllis. You're ready.'

Get Ready is a state of mind, kind of like Sheryl Sandberg's *Lean In*. It's about dealing with adversity and knocking down those barriers of gender, ethnicity, and so on. The key is not to do it alone. Instead, have someone amazing in your corner right alongside you, helping you.

Nelson Mandela was an inspiration to me, too. His life story is about having a cause greater than himself: social justice. Great leaders, whom I admire, always have a cause, a purpose greater than themselves. If you work for a company, you better believe in it. The best leaders know and live the values of the company because they are the same values with which they live their lives. They know why they're doing what they're doing and they know what legacy they want to leave.

My cause is developing great leaders. I want to make sure leaders are the best they can be, so the company is better and so the community is better. I sit on boards so I can have influence and help the company or organization shape its culture. I want to create a better society.

MAVERON
DAN LEVITAN, MANAGING PARTNER

DEAL WITH THE 800-POUND GORILLA

There are four people who've had an impact on me. First, I would say Howard Schultz, CEO of Starbucks, and my partner in Maveron. He's impacted me through his infectious passion for everything he does – his persistence in trying to be the best at whatever it is and his unbridled aspiration.

Second is Coach Mike Kryzysewki (Coach K), the winningest coach in college basketball history. He's the head coach of men's basketball at Duke University, my alma mater, and coach of the gold medal-winning US men's Olympic basketball team. He's taught me what it takes to build a program – as opposed to a team – and the importance of process, discipline and focus. When Duke goes out to play, we play 40 minutes with the same process, discipline and focus – whether we're up by 50, down by 50, or tied. There are rules of conduct of what it means to be part of his team, and I'm trying to incorporate some of that into our culture.

Next is Bill Campbell, chairman of the board at Intuit. He's known as Silicon Valley's coach. He's coached Steve Jobs and Erik Schmidt of Google, among others. Bill taught me loyalty. He has an incredible sense of loyalty and commitment to finishing the job and to taking a long-term view of success.

Last is Joel Peterson, chairman of the board of Jet Blue. Joel taught me to tell the truth always. Many years ago, I had Joel come in and observe Maveron. I asked him for this thoughts and he wrote me an eight-page missive. I liked it, but wanted to edit a few things before I sent it to the team. He said, 'If you want to edit a few things, don't send it to your team. It's either all or none.' He taught me to be honest and transparent: You put the 800-pound gorilla on the table, and you deal with it.

NBC KING 5
RAY HEACOX, PRESIDENT & GENERAL MANAGER

BE A GOOD THINKER

As early as high school, I experienced a foundational change in who I was and who I would become. I was destined to choose a path that fit my quiet, reserved, introverted personality, until I decided to step out of the box and join the high school debate team.

I got scholarship assistance to go to Pacific Lutheran University and compete on the debate team. Theodore O. H. Karl was the chairman of the communications department and encouraged me to join. Karl was a legend as a debate coach; he taught me logic for making good arguments and the speech skills to use that logic. Our team worked really hard and we ended up becoming very competitive at a national level; that helped me to think fast and strategically.

Overall, I'd describe my leadership as an amalgam of people and source material, which taught me to be a good thinker and strategist and to conceptualize problems.

I admire the Dalai Lama most, not the typical business leaders. Someone like the Dalai Lama leads from a position of service and has been able to do important things in the world without flexing power over anyone else. My attraction to such leaders is a response to the decade I spent at NBC, which General Electric owned. At the time, Jack Welch was at the helm. GE was unbelievably great at investing in and developing business leaders and having bench talent. I thought Welch was brilliant in many ways – he provided absolute clarity of direction. But there were negative aspects to the culture, too; I didn't buy into the 'eat or be eaten' mentality of extreme competition.

OKI GOLF AND OKI DEVELOPMENTS, INC.
SCOTT OKI, FOUNDER & CHAIRMAN

GET OUT OF YOUR COMFORT ZONE

For me, lessons in leadership started early. I grew up in the inner city of Seattle, and we didn't have much money. When I was 13 years old, I was a Boy Scout and our troop was part of the Buddhist church. My parents let me use a little bit of money to join the drum and bugle corps of the Boy Scouts. I played saxophone at school and wanted to play the bugle. Harry Hammond, our music director, said it would ruin my embouchure, but he said I could play drums. So I started playing the drums and I got pretty good at it. Mr. Hammond was also the music director for the Shriners' drum and bugle corps, and he convinced me to give lessons at night to the 'old guys' who played the drums in the Shriners' band. By giving lessons and interacting with these guys, I got out of my comfort zone. I realized, 'If I can do this, there are a lot of other things I can do.' And ever since, I've believed there is very little I can't do.

I don't think there's one leader I identify with; I identify with a lot of individuals. Bill Gates is a perfect example. He's someone who was totally passionate about writing software – and is now unbelievably passionate about philanthropy. I don't know what Bill's I.Q. is, but it's at least 100 points above mine. I'll never be as smart as Bill and probably will never work as hard as Bill. So to see someone who has done such amazing things in the areas he's passionate about is very instructive. I look to people like Bill, who are students of everything.

PROJECT BIONIC
JOSH DIRKS, CO-FOUNDER & CEO

LET PEOPLE FAIL

I was very fortunate to have several mentors. Randy Riddell owned a sandwich chain that he let me help run when I was really young. Randy empowered me to do anything and everything in his organization. He even let me fail at times – and then taught me how to learn from those failures. Randy also taught me to be transparent and candid about my own personal goals and direction in my life.

Karl Kohler, whom I worked with at Door to Door, was another mentor in my life. He taught me the importance of corporate communication and how you build a culture. The funny thing was that Karl wasn't 'that guy,' but through our osmosis, we both became better leaders. My business partner today, Jason Richards, taught me how to be humble and how to support and drive our values with a clear mission. In the two years he's been with our organization he's had a dramatic impact.

I'm a big sports person, and I identify with a cadre of sports leaders. Phil Jackson is one of the greatest coaches in the history of the NBA. I admire him because he had a lot of prima donna personalities that he had to bring together as a team. He was a puppet master or an orchestrator who kept out of the middle of things, and that strategy allowed him to have amazing success.

Retired Miami Dolphins coach Don Shula was one of the winningest coaches of all time because he knew how to create a culture in which people looked forward to being at work every day. Also, Robert Kiyosaki, author of *Rich Dad, Poor Dad*, influenced me in terms of how you change your thought processes and patterns to get yourself to achieve your life goals.

Someone I look up to who's running a big company is Marisa Mayer, CEO of Yahoo. I've found her to be very motivating because she doesn't apologize for some of the risks she takes. At the same time, she takes input from employees and is willing to make the hard decisions in real time. Her risks have paid off with an upward-climbing stock price. I admire her for the way she's pivoting that company and brand.

SEATTLE METROPOLITAN CHAMBER OF COMMERCE
MAUD DAUDON, CEO

TURN PEOPLE INTO BELIEVERS

My parents have been two great models. My father was incredibly thoughtful, inclusive and an equitable person. He was a lawyer, very intellectually astute. He taught me how to have the facts and figures lined up behind my opinions. My mom was smart and community minded with a powerful personality. She volunteered with great organizations and raised three daughters and one son, all of whom have become dynamic leaders in their own right.

My first mentor in my first job was a contractor by trade, and a self-made millionaire, who chaired a citizen's commission I staffed. We would get together and he would teach me something – it could be negotiation skills, it could be strategy. He had an incredibly generous spirit and would do this on his own time and of his own volition. He was smart and strategic and told me to go get a business degree, 'because this is what you do know – and this is what you *don't* know.'

When I served as deputy mayor, Mayor Paul Schell was another important person in my leadership development. He saw the future in an interesting way and integrated that into a vision and strategy. During our administration, we saw the violence of the World Trade Organization (WTO) event, Boeing move its headquarters out of Washington State and the dot-com bubble burst. I learned the value of intellectual capital and compassion. I learned to apply systems thinking across a whole community. I learned the meaning of unconditional loyalty. Once you earned his respect, there was nothing you could do to shake it. If he believed in you, he would do anything he could to help support you.

After reading *Team of Rivals*, the leader I admire most is Abraham Lincoln. I learned that he surrounded himself with his former adversaries. They challenged his thinking, yet he managed to keep his own thoughts and leadership intact. He kept his own counsel and based his decisions on his own moral values. He was a concise and precise communicator, who possessed a wonderful sense of humor even during incredible adversity.

SEATTLE FOUNDATION
NORM RICE, PRESIDENT & CEO

LOSING TEACHES MORE THAN WINNING

I don't think I had a true mentor as I moved along, especially since a predominant part of my life has been in elected office. Elected office is much different from corporate life. Clearly, my elected leadership played a big role in shaping who I am, and what I do. The biggest influence on me was losing elections, rather than winning. I learned more about why I lost than why I won. If you don't know your core values – the things that are your moral compass – I think you'll fail. I remember a former manager telling me, 'We always knew your values.' My values were:

- Social equity

- Economic opportunity

- Environmental stewardship

We designed whatever we pursued to enhance those standards and the values served as a good guidepost. It allowed everyone to come back to the core beliefs that were guiding the administration. I don't think that's too different from any other organization, but sometimes we get so caught up in a bottom-line mentality that we forget the value of the overarching organization and the value to its constituency or customers.

I admire a lot of people, and they've changed as I've gotten older. Heroes are different than leaders. The value of someone like Nelson Mandela is the ability to stay the course despite the adversity, which is different than leading an organization for profitability. The achievements are not the same. I ask myself, 'What did they do that I would like to do and achieve in the same way to be successful?'

SEATTLE UNIVERSITY
FATHER STEPHEN SUNDBORG, PRESIDENT

GO FORWARD AND TAKE IT ON

Jim Sinegal, co-founder and retired CEO of Costco, had a big impact on me as a leader. Jim was on the board here for 16 years, and was the chair of the board for four years. I've never known a CEO who headed such a major corporation and is so straightforward, has absolute integrity and loves what he does. He has had an enormous influence on me.

So has Pedro Arrupe, who was the superior general of the Jesuits from 1965-83. As the head of the Jesuits, he led the charge to really confront the modern world. He had a strong 'let's go forward, let's take it on' attitude. And he was from the Basque region of Spain, so he had that fiery inspiration. I started as a Jesuit in 1961. At just the right time, in my middle years, Arrupe came along and inspired me to realize there's a lot I could do. He was generous, bright, culturally engaged, a dynamic kind of person. He did most of his work in Japan and was there, with eight other Jesuits, in 1945 when the US dropped the atomic bomb. All eight survived and he used his medical skills to help the thousands of wounded. He was an international figure and passed away in 1991.

SPECIAL OLYMPICS OF WASHINGTON
BETH WOJICK, PRESIDENT & CEO

THINK BIG, CELEBRATE SUCCESS

Bob Gobrecht was the CEO of Seafair and my first boss out of college. He took me with him when he went to the Mariners to be the vice president of sales. Now, I'm working for him for the third time. He's the regional president of North America for Special Olympics, and he asked me to come be the CEO of our state chapter. Bob taught me to be a visionary, to think big. He also taught me to celebrate success. He taught me to always check contracts – which most people don't seem to do. I love the way Bob talks to me; he makes me believe I can do huge things.

Chuck Armstrong, former CEO of the Mariners, was another person who had a significant impact on my leadership. He's a very smart and demanding leader. I learned a lot. As the first female director of corporate marketing in all of baseball, I was the only woman at the Mariners with an office. Chuck never saw me as anything other than a capable leader. For the four years I was there, he challenged me just as much as he challenged everyone else.

Hillary Clinton has been my role model since I read her autobiography. She graduated number one in her class from Yale Law School; she's a force in her own right even though she could have bowed to her husband's position as president. When I was younger, Margaret Thatcher also inspired me. She played on the world stage against some very powerful foes, such as Mikhail Gorbachev.

Locally, Phyllis Campbell of JP Morgan Chase is someone I admire. She's rock solid, that woman. She's unflappable, with good ethics and a solid foundation.

The best thing about my job, and throughout my career, is that I've had the opportunity to get advice and counsel from some very important people. At Seafair, I had great people around me. At the Mariners, I worked with the ownership group to help design Safeco Field. Here, at Special Olympics, I've worked with an incredible board of directors who all bring great things to the party. I'm so lucky to have had these opportunities.

STE. MICHELLE WINE ESTATES
TED BASELER, PRESIDENT & CEO

BE A GENTLEMAN

I was fortunate to work with a collection of outstanding people early in my career. I worked with passionate people at renowned advertising firm J. Walter Thompson in Chicago. And at Cole & Weber in Seattle, the people were inspirational and demonstrated such integrity; it made me want to work harder.

The person I've been most impressed with is Pierro Antinori, pre-eminent Italian winemaker and businessmen. Antinori personifies being a gentleman. He's smart and articulate, but doesn't show off. He's a tough business genius, but doesn't put it in people's faces. He's innovative and has exquisite taste, which is a combination of incredible attributes. If I could model just 20% of his behavior I'd be a better leader.

Of the great leaders I've read about, I most admire Abe Lincoln. He was very clever, and I think it was clear he knew how to get things done. He didn't give up when Congress was fighting him. He just figured out ways to work the system to reach his goals. He was an outstanding listener and would sit with people one on one and listen and challenge them. When you think about what he accomplished in such a difficult time, it's probably unprecedented.

TOM DOUGLAS RESTAURANTS
PAMELA HINCKLEY, CEO

STAY STRONG IN THE FACE OF ADVERSITY

I cut my teeth at Redhook Brewery and spent 15 years working with Paul Shipman, founder and president. I was fortunate to join Redhook in the early days, and I watched the company grow and evolve.

Paul had a cult passion for the beer business and was a formally trained business student. He created a partnership with Anheuser-Busch, took us through an initial public offering (IPO) and expanded to the East Coast. It was an interesting exercise in merging two very different cultures. Paul was great at considering all angles before making a decision. I learned perseverance and to stay strong and hold on to my values in the face of adversity.

Tom Douglas and I have been friends for 35 years, and I've watched how he's grown the business. When I was at Redhook, Tom helped me open our Fremont facility and develop the food program. As the godmother of his daughter, I was babysitting when the Dahlia Lounge opened. When I decided to leave my job at Theo's Chocolates, Tom added the position of CEO and asked me to come on board. I was pretty thrilled, and over the last four years in this position, I've watched and participated in all that he and Jackie Cross, his wife and business partner, have built and continue to create.

There are other leaders I admire too, starting with John Kerry. I'm from the East Coast and have a Boston bias. I was in college during the Vietnam War, and Kerry was one of the first politicians to question U.S. involvement. I think that says a lot about a person who served in the military, and had the sense to question military operations. Now he's willing to dig into the Middle East and try to bring a fresh approach. I think that says a lot about his leadership.

I love that President Obama came out of the grassroots/activism community and hoped it would apply in Washington, DC. It's fascinating that the issues he's chosen to focus on as president are truly the issues that are most important to him. Healthcare isn't the issue that wins friends; that's climate change. He's chosen to focus on the few things that matter most, make them priorities and stay diligent. He's doing what a leader has to do, which doesn't pave the path to popularity, but is what's best for the country.

Kurt Dammeier, owner of Beecher's Handmade Cheese is someone I don't know well, but when I've interacted with him, I'm impressed by the good and hard questions he asks. He's got his fingers in quite a few things, and we've had several conversations about brand building, which is my favorite subject. One of my goals this year is to pick his brain a little more. I love how he's tied Beecher's to a live production facility and really given it a sense of product origin.

UW MEDICINE, DR. PAUL RAMSEY
CEO AND DEAN OF THE SCHOOL OF MEDICINE

TAKE LEADERSHIP LESSONS FROM ROWING

I was fortunate to have several key mentors over the course of my career. One was Dr. Phillip Fialkow, who was my direct boss twice and held this job before I did. All my mentors gave me their time, their advice, their feedback, and in different ways served as role models for me. They were straightforward, honest, and demonstrated integrity and accountability. Although I am different from each of them, each had an impact on my learning. The *New York Times* quoted me last summer saying that my best teacher was Harry Parker, who was my rowing coach in college. Although the 'curriculum' he taught was rowing, he taught me teamwork, individual accountability and continuous process improvement.

I have spent time with some of the world's best-known leaders, including Nelson Mandela and three U.S. presidents. I draw inspiration from a number of people considered national and international leaders in several ways. Within our community, I've been fortunate to work with leaders like Jerry Grinstein, who served in several major leadership roles, including as CEO of Delta Air Lines. Jerry has an amazing ability to combine astute cognition, reflection and compassion with a wonderful sense of humor. This combination of qualities provides a model for me to attempt to make wise decisions about strategic options. It has been a privilege for me to work with Jerry and to attempt to learn from him.

XTREME CONSULTING
GREG RANKICH, CEO

HIRE SMART PEOPLE

I grew up watching my dad run his company. He treated everyone who worked for him like family and they were always at our family functions. I was about 10 years old before I realized that some of his employees weren't our relatives. Even when he was mad, he'd still hug it out and they'd still be part of the family. I try to do that here at my company. I try to know everyone on different levels, know their spouses or boyfriends, or girlfriends. It's hard to maintain that as we grow, but it's important and I try hard.

Entrepreneurship is in my DNA. When I was a kid, I had a lemonade stand and realized I could sell more by opening earlier and selling doughnuts and coffee. My dad and my godfather would talk business, and I would listen and really pay attention. One of the best lessons I learned was to hire smart people. In the early years of Xtreme, I asked my dad a lot of questions, and our conversations kept coming back to that. I've made sure to hire smart people, whom I know I can completely trust. For example, our lawyer changed firms three times, so we've changed firms three times. I trust her and will stick with her no matter where she goes.

My godfather, Milan Panić, is someone I really admire. He came from Yugoslavia with basically nothing. He founded a huge pharmaceuticals company that became publicly traded. In the early '90s, he was prime minister of the Federal Republic of Yugoslavia, and ran for president but lost to Slobodan Milosevic. Growing up, I idolized him. He was self-made, and I internalized that value. My parents were upper middle class, but I never asked for anything from them, other than advice.

COMMON EXPERIENCES

Are there lessons here? I love the question, 'If you could have dinner with three people, dead or alive, who would they be?' These stories gave me a whole lot more people to consider. I mean, it's not often that you hear Abraham Lincoln, Jean Valjean and Phil Jackson discussed as if they should all be sitting at the same table. But clearly they could be. There are threaded themes of common ground in these answers. Like me, many of the leaders I spoke with were inspired and shaped by their parents. Like me, most had mentors (like Mike) who were very influential in their development. Although Abraham Lincoln is the inspirational figure cited most often, what struck me is that even when leaders cited other people as influences, they often praised similar qualities:

- Determination in the face of adversity and chaos
- The ability to have people with different personalities and opinions (even antagonists) work well together
- The will to hold strong to core values under the most challenging circumstances
- The grace to treat everyone – regardless of title or status – as someone worthy of attention and respect
- Humility

It can't be an accident that these qualities come up again and again. But if these qualities are the backbone of great leadership (and it seems they are) it also seems fair to ask why they are so rare in business today. Take a second to think about those who've influenced your leadership.

IN YOUR OWN WORDS

1.   Who had a key impact on *you* as a leader? Why?

_____

_____

_____

2.   Of all the famous leaders you know or have read about, with whom do you most identify and why?

_____

_____

_____

3.   Which of the leaders' answers most surprise you?

_____

_____

_____

4.   Have you served as mentor to a future leader? If so, what do you think were the most important things you imparted?

_____

_____

_____

5.   If you haven't yet been a mentor, could you be? What are the most significant lessons you would like to instill?

_____

_____

_____

PART 2: GENERATIONAL ANGST

WHAT'S THE FIRST RULE OF FIGHT CLUB?

Quick! Which is the best movie: *Casablanca*, *The Graduate*, *Fight Club* or *The Matrix*? Your answer is almost certainly determined by your generation. And if you're like most people, you believe that not only is the movie you picked clearly the best, but the others are somewhere between tedious and inane.

Like it or not, we are products of our generations. When it comes to talking movies, that can be either baffling or amusing, depending on your mood. But when it comes to working together, it can also be irritating, frustrating, infuriating … you get the idea. And that's a problem with four generations, nearly five, currently working (or trying to) side by side in today's organizations. This is the first time in history that we've had such a multi-generational workforce.

With a wide range of opinions, knowledge, values, expectations and demands bubbling in the cubicle cauldron, companies face an urgent need to develop leaders at all levels: To bring younger leaders online faster, to develop leaders globally and to keep senior leaders relevant and engaged longer.[1] Therein lies the challenge for leaders. There *are* important generational differences, and we can't talk about leadership without noting them.

This book contains perspectives from members of the Greatest Generation, the Baby Boomers, Generation X and Generation Y (Millennials). And to better understand each other's collective culture, I'm a fan of enlisting pop culture. Let's go to the movies.

For example, it's hard not to see *Casablanca* (1942) as the embodiment of the Greatest Generation's outlook: Idealism trumps cynicism, self-sacrifice trumps romance, and commitment to a noble cause trumps all. As Humphrey Bogart says to Ingrid Bergman (spoiler alert!) at the end of the movie, "It doesn't take much to see that the problems of three little people don't amount to a hill of beans in this crazy world."

The Graduate (1967), *Easy Rider* (1969) and *The Big Chill* (1983) are all about Boomers and all share themes of anti-authority, lost idealism and squandered opportunities. The all-encompassing *Forrest Gump* (1994) ties up all the historical milestones that defined the Baby Boomer's generation with a nice bow: The JFK assassination, the Civil Rights movement, Vietnam, sex, drugs, rock 'n' roll and Watergate.

The irony for Gen X is that they hate being defined and "joining" is absolutely out of the question. Yet the standout movies were all about "clubs," so to speak. *The Breakfast Club* (1985) defined fashion, slang and the need to break out of the social hierarchy and redefine arbitrary rules laid down by parents and teachers. *Fight Club* (1999) went further. It challenged the Gen X stereotype as apathetic, flannel-wearing, grunge-listening slackers. Instead, the film argued that it's not a lack of passion that kept those in their late twenties to early thirties befuddled, but a lack of personal power, a lack of freedom – the impotence of not knowing your *real* soul[2].

Finally, Millennials. Look at *The Hunger Games* (2012), and let's call it what it is, a movie about kids killing kids. That's not the best recipe for creating a sustainable society, but what do I know? No one's beating down my door to buy my film rights. Beyond *The Hunger Games*, we've also seen *The Matrix* and *The Social Network*. *The Matrix* (1999) touched on the most basic of Gen Y ideology, their dependence on technology and their uncertainty about the world. Why are we here? How can we change things? Why are things the way they are? The answers are literally at their fingertips. *Rolling Stone* summarizes *The Social Network* (2010) perfectly: The movie shows "how technology is winning the battle against actual human contact, creating a nation of narcissists shaping their own reality just like a Facebook page."[3]

I mentioned earlier that my oldest sister is 19 years older than I am. There are two more siblings between us, who I haven't mentioned. My brother is 17 years older, and another sister is 13 years older than I am. Given that I come from a multi-generational family, I had a lot of exposure to a range of culture at a pretty young age. And I think one of the best ways to find context and common ground is by understanding the lexicon of movies, especially those that rise up as the iconic voice for each generation. "What's the first Rule of Fight Club?" Exactly.

Going forward in the workforce, what kind of leaders will we need? Will we get those kinds of leaders? No one really has the answers to those questions yet, but to fully understand the situation let's look at the generations and how the differences manifest at work.

GENERATIONS DEFINED

Generational labeling is nothing new. The Greatests did it to the Boomers, the Boomers to the Gen Xers, and so forth. In fact, it's thought that Socrates said: "Our youth now love luxury. They have bad manners, contempt for authority; they show disrespect for their elders and love chatter in place of exercise; they no longer rise when elders enter the room; they contradict their parents, chatter before company; gobble up their food and tyrannize their teachers."

Every generation has thought the one after it lacks morals, lacks respect for authority, and lacks motivation. The leaders in this book span the generation spectrum, and for clarification, here's a brief summary of what that means in the workforce.

The Greatest Generation

A handful of interviewees fall into what journalist Tom Brokaw called "The Greatest Generation," referring to those born before 1946 and also known as the Mature/WWII Generation. Although most members have retired from the labor force, they comprise a wealth of valuable knowledge and experience. Many believe this generation views work as an obligation: they respect authority, take rational approaches, and produce quality work.[4]

Baby Boomers

Predictably, the majority of leaders I interviewed fall into the Baby Boomer generation, born between 1946 and 1965. I say predict-ably because this generation now occupies most of the senior-level management roles. They are often stereotyped as wanting to change the world and being extremely focused on work. They possess a strong work ethic and want to be recognized for their efforts.[5] The older members have begun to retire from the labor force, a significant factor in the growing leadership gap.

Generation X

Those born between 1966 and 1980 are categorized as Gen X. The oldest members could now be entering senior-level management roles, while the younger members are approaching mid-career and senior-level supervisory roles.[6] Many members of Gen X embrace diversity[7] and entrepreneurship. They are unimpressed with authority and titles and looked for competence in leaders. They take a balanced approach to work and life. Full disclosure: I am a Gen Xer.

Millennials

Millennials (or Gen Y) are defined as the generation born 1981-1995. Many are just entering the workforce, and others have two to three years under their belts. They look for companies with good reputations and ethics, that have cultural diversity and are technology savvy corporations. As the generational low man on the workforce totem pole, Millennials are often pegged as entitled and self-absorbed.

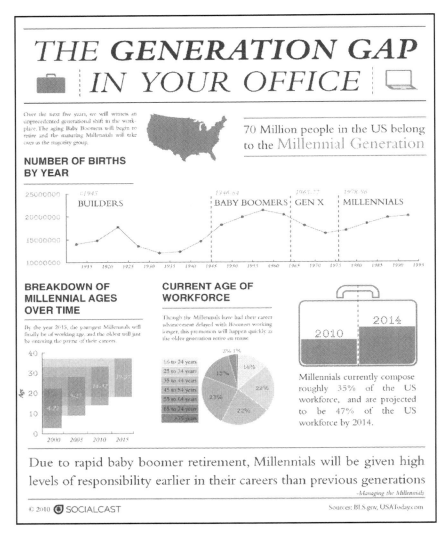

Source: InfoGraphics.

http://infographics.idlelist.com/2012/10/31/the-generation-gap-in-your-office/

PERCEPTION IS REALITY

Doting Baby Boomer parents raised Millennials in prosperous economic times and placed them on pedestals. One of the consistent threads in nearly all of the conversations was the subtle (or not so subtle) opinion of the up-and-coming workforce. In that context, they've been described as overly ambitious dreamers who don't want to pay their dues and are only concerned about higher pay and more time off. At the same time, they're thought to be a group that takes collective action and who are optimistic about the future. Based on what I heard about this up-and-coming group, many leaders agree – if not strongly agree – with all sides of this depiction.

Most experts see the differences in generations as largely style and priorities. But they also see that Millennials are set apart from the previous generations because of technology. As well, two of the strongest traditional contributors to success – education and values – have been neglected. Just as in *The Social Network*, a critical difference for Millennials is that technology is an integrated part of their world. It's a language in which they are highly proficient; so proficient, in fact, that they don't know life without it. Still, in all the research I've read, the unanswered question about Millennials is whether they will be the best or worst generation yet; the anticipation is killing me. Let's look at the reasons why the jury is still out.

A SLOW GLOBAL ASS-KICKING

Nothing says obvious outcome like cause and effect. Everyone has an opinion on the wrong and right ways to educate: Flip the classroom, give kids autonomy, blah blah blah. Before changing careers, I worked for an education technology company that develops digital curriculum for high school students. As head of corporate communications, I got to dive into the depths of education reform and see first-hand how hard it is to turn a tree that's hundreds of years old.

If education continues to fail our kids in the beginning, their chances of achieving their highest potential are low. And we are fu… (we'll say limited.)

And to continue on the finger-pointing track, a quick call out to Helicopter Parents (a.k.a., Boomers): You didn't do your kids (or our society) much of a service when you created a culture of trophy-getters instead of real winners. You know who you are. And everyone knows the story, so I'll be brief.

Somehow the minimum standard of doing your best every time you step up to the plate got lost in a deflation of values. You can disagree, but let me throw out the numbers: 34, 26, 21, 17.[8]

- 34 is the number of member countries in the Organization for Economic Co-operation and Development (OECD), the international survey that evaluates education systems worldwide.
- 26th is where US students rank in mathematics. Below average, indeed. Shanghai ranks first.
- 17th is where the US ranks in reading. Average.
- 21st is where the US ranks in science. Shanghai, Hong Kong, Singapore, Japan and Finland are the top five performers in science.

In addition, while research tells us more kids are going to college, it also states that more students are coming out of colleges and universities unprepared for the workplace.

The data indicates that this generation is "starting adult life with less knowledge."[9] The onus to bridge this gap falls on the part of employers, through training, coaching and mentoring. An article in *Fast Company* claims that more than 50% of business leaders say

Millennials lack the professional skills needed for even entry-level positions.[10]

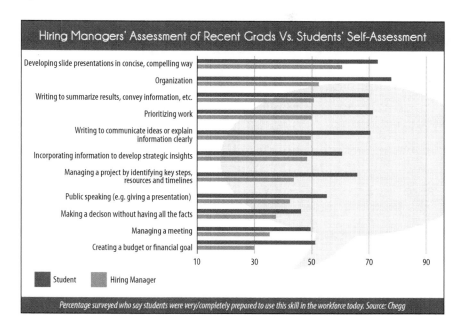

Source: Qualified in Their Own Minds, Inside Higher Ed, October 29, 2013, http://www.insidehighered.com/news/2013/10/29/ more-data-show-students-unprepared-work-what-do-about-it

And there's more. Beyond lacking the necessary workplace skills, Millennials have worrisome traits that differ from their predecessors. A study by Bersin & Associates showed that Millennials had lower scores in altruism, coupled with higher narcissism, assertiveness[11], self-esteem[12] and individualistic traits in general[13] than previous generations. The trend is toward a confident – albeit self-serving – talent pool.

So, while kids in China, Singapore, Japan and Finland are kicking our future's intellectual butt, as a country we've rewarded average and we're paying the price. When average is what we strive for, we can't help but get what we deserve. Right now, that's a slow, global ass-kicking.

However, when kids strive to do better than their personal best, the rubber meets the road. That's what leaders are made of. Doing better than your best – or at least trying to – sets you on a trajectory to want more, work harder and achieve at your highest level. Remember that silly mindset called competition? Like math, I consider competition to be a universal truth. And I'm certain that anyone who rises through the ranks to leader, in whatever capacity, has trashed his or her pile of worthless trophies. Our values are what add value; there's no way around it.

DIFFERING PERSPECTIVES ON MILLENNIALS

You can't have a discussion about emerging leaders without singling out the up-and-coming generation. And that's where the commonality ends.

In Beth Wojick's role as CEO of Special Olympics, her work with young people is unique. Based on her observations and interactions, Wojick sees Millennials as having some additional work to do.

"The generation entering the workforce now has a really different work ethic. They don't think the way we did in terms of moving up and I don't think they know what Dress for Success is. These young adults think that success is something they deserve. They deserve the business card, the title, and the office. And you don't see the extra effort.

"This is the group where everyone got a trophy for showing up. Parents were making good money and half of these kids still live at home. When I ask this group to name their role models, they can't see past mom and dad. When I ask where they get their news, they tell me Twitter in 140 characters. They know the headlines, but can't talk about the depth of the story or the issue. I've made reading the business sections of the major papers a required part of their job."

John Rubino, of Green Rubino, agrees. "Millennials have a different perspective on careers and work than I did when I was 27 years old. Their expectations and sense of entitlement are barriers. They think things should just come to them, versus working hard for what they want. They have a now, now, now mentality that's just not realistic," he says.

In fact, Millennials' impatience is an issue that came up again and again during the interviews. "I love the enthusiasm, the candid spirit and optimism that young talent brings to the table, but you don't just get a promotion right away," says Phyllis Campbell of JP Morgan Chase. She suggests that younger leaders, "Think about how you can be the best at your job and then find ways to make your best even better. Becoming a leader takes time."

Clearly, Millennials' sense of entitlement bugs people. But there's more to it than just being irritating. "Young high potentials think they know it all, and they stretch beyond their competence, which can be dangerous," says ICHS' Teresita Batayola.

Most of the beefs against the Millennials focus on the impact their need for instant gratification can have on an organization. But as Maveron's Dan Levitan sees it, that impatience can also create problems for themselves. "Some Millennials can't look at careers in the fullness of time," he says. "They think in short-term spans. As I see it, when you think about a career, you start with the end in mind and work backwards. You don't worry that, 'I wasn't productive this month.' If you're in the right organization, if you have the right mentors, if there are great leaders around you who you're learning from then you don't leave if you have one or two months where you don't feel it's been as powerful as before. Great organizations have longevity – whether it's business, sports teams, you name it, there's some continuity piece that works. No doubt about it. I've had two jobs since business school, one for 14 years in investment banking and this one."

It seems unlikely that many Millennials will shape their career from two jobs. In fact, the opposite seems inevitable: "I heard recently, maybe on NPR, that the up-and-coming generation will have an average of 27 jobs," says Scott Oki of Oki Developments. "If that's true, that begs the question, can they make the commitment that I'm looking for? And what does that mean for the success or failure of any number of companies? I think that will be a big challenge for up-and-coming leaders."

Paradoxically, another challenge is that while some Millennials may feel unreasonably entitled, others don't see their own potential. "There are so many young people with potential, but often they're unfocused and wild. Sometimes they don't settle down and it takes them far longer to get it," Batayola adds. "The challenge is identifying those worth developing."

Although he sees the behavior that other leaders associate with Millennials, Dan Price of Gravity Payments (at 29, the only Millennial I interviewed) isn't inclined to label it a generational issue. "In the early stages of life or adulthood, you kind of hop around and jump from one thing to another and don't have a lot of commitment or attachment," he says. "That's a trend now that I think is partially generationally driven, but partially enabled by technology. I think people overhype the generational aspect of it. A lot of it is just the way the world is. Technology enables us to do things more quickly; we dive in more quickly and in some ways achieve competence in a deeper, faster way.

"There's more temptation in life today, too – more than ever before. Advertising has been around for hundreds of years, but today it's explicitly sexual and over-consuming. The message of 'do this thing – and you will be prosperous and life will be easy' is constantly fed to us. And that message is reinforced in other ways, too. My younger brother is a psych major, and he was in a class or reading something and he pointed out that porn and video games provide instant gratification like never before. You train your brain to get that gratification without having to do anything. And I think that's dangerous because your brain is very trainable. You want to develop habits that lead to a long, happy, fulfilling life, not a life of instant gratification."

HAPPINESS IN CHANGEVILLE

The Project Bionic staff of 16 is mostly made up of Millennials and Josh Dirks' observations are far more optimistic.

"Millennials bring a fresh perspective. They choose actions that are good for the whole; collective concepts like car sharing, micro-housing, micro-donations are resonating and thriving with this new audience. They are adaptive to new ideas, technologies, and ways of doing things. Not only do they not mind change, often they demand it. They break rules and question authority. While some may see this as a negative, the new generation is happy to challenge the norm. They've seen corporate America ruin their parents and thus will question and challenge why things are done in the ways that they are. Many of the thought leaders of this generation are building new ways of banking, connecting, and using resources that are finite.

"How do these traits help business leaders today? First they bring a unique perspective to the workplace. Managers can throw these young people into new projects or move them around without fearing they will explode in Changeville. These young people will bring solutions to the table no one has thought of before.

"Their expectations are lower. While this may contradict the entitlement Millennials are known for, Millennials have seen their parents lose their retirement funds, have friends that have college degrees who can't find jobs, and many have been forced to go back home and live with their parents. Thus, their expectations have been greatly diminished about the world going forward. However, I believe they generally have a desire to help everyone make the workforce of tomorrow a gold mine of strong minds and values."

Josh Dirks isn't the only one who has hope for the future. If she doesn't yet fully appreciate the Millennials' perspective, Beth Wojick does have praise for the generation behind them. "The good news is, that the kids in high schools right now, are fantastic!" she says. "This high school generation has ethics maybe like the Greatest Generation had. They support our Special Olympic athletes in unique ways, making sure that we are included in Unified Sports, Unified Dances and other in-school activities. They are incredibly hard working and they 'get it.' I'm not sure what changed here, probably parenting and economics."

KALEIDOSCOPE OF CHANGE

That said, we're in a kaleidoscope of change, and transformation is happening at a faster pace than we've ever seen. Some leaders I spoke with recognized the value of the Millennials' tech savviness and ability to adapt at warp speed. However, they are very concerned that the sense of individual entitlement and need for constant attention will hinder Millennial success in the traditional work culture.

But the traditional culture is also up for debate. All the leaders I interviewed recognize the environment is changing, and no one knows how it will look in the next 10 years. As we continue to maneuver such fluidity, a collision of minds is inevitable. Current leaders will need to recognize this new generation's fresh and different ways of thinking, and the Millennials will need to step up their game.

As Phyllis Campbell notes, "It's up to us, as leaders, to listen to the ideas of the good thinking of the younger generation. These up-and-comers are our next leaders – and they have interesting thoughts on how to do things differently. This is the generation of our future – future leaders and future customers. Our challenge is to listen and mine the best thinking."

But Teresita Batayola cautions against focusing *all* future thinking on younger employees. "We have to focus on developing leaders of all ages, not just young people who stand out as high-potentials," she says. "Seasoned workers bring to the organization a life experience that young people just don't have. Maybe those seasoned people are not in formal leadership positions. There are informational leaders; there are moral leaders. We have a nurse who is truly a moral leader. She stepped up when we were going through a major transition to electronic medical records. Employees continue to look up to her, but she made it clear that her passion is dealing with patients and that's what she wants to do. Even though she's not taking on 'leadership,' I have to continue to ensure that people like her are nurtured."

But leaders aren't the only ones who will need a broader perspective. Millennials will need to put on their big boy and big girl underpants if they want to be taken seriously. Expecting to sit at the table because you showed up doesn't fly. A seat is not a right, it's earned. And, once a seat at the table is earned, it's a fantastic learning opportunity – if you're listening. As my mentor told me: If you're talking, you're not listening and if you're not listening you're not learning.

Earning the opportunity to be heard means you have something to say that adds value, which honestly is always the goal. To be recognized as a smart, original thinker means you work hard to differentiate yourself and bring the best ideas to the table. Half-baked creativity gained kudos from your parents, but doesn't fly in the boardroom – any boardroom, even if the CEO is 22. At a minimum, that means taking time to learn, listen and comprehend more than 140 characters of 'news' and actually develop the skills and tools to earn a promotion. Some of the leaders I spoke with named these as huge challenges. And as many of them emphasized, leadership requires ongoing learning. It doesn't happen overnight or in a two-week course. Here, take a moment to think about your own leadership. How do you as a leader (or aspiring leader) think about generational differences and how do you plan to maximize them?

IN YOUR OWN WORDS

1.   Which of the stereotypes about your generation are true of you? (Be honest)

_____

_____

_____

2.   What bugs you most about other generations? How can you resolve those differences or change those perceptions?

_____

_____

_____

3.   What have you or can you learn from other generations?

_____

_____

_____

4.   As a leader, what can you do to bring different generations together?

_____

_____

_____

5.   How might generational differences affect the future of your organization? What can you do now to build a stronger future?

_____

_____

_____

PART 3: FROM THEIR PERSPECTIVE: DEFINING LEADERSHIP

That annoying kid who asked, "Why?" after every answer given to her? Yes, that kid was me (and probably everyone else in this book). The trouble is, as an adult I never broke that habit. It just intensified. It wasn't uncommon for people to leave a meeting with me feeling they'd just been interrogated. (And yes, that included dates.)

Now the questions I ask as a writer and coach still make some people slightly uncomfortable, but it makes me really good at what I do. Ask any of my clients. In writing this book, I was privileged to ask some of our best leaders tough questions. I was amazed at the array of answers. In some ways, asking a bunch of experts how they define leadership is a bit like asking them to describe the mystery meat on a menu: It seems simple in theory, but some talk about the texture, others focus on taste. I decided to break it down bite by bite. And while I heard about planning strategically, communicating a vision, and making decisions, the more I listened, the juicier things got. I quickly realized that those competencies – while certainly important – are only half the story.

Half the story is about the *how* of leadership; the other half is about the *why*. While supervisors and managers at all levels of the organization communicate, make decisions and, to some extent, determine strategy, something greater sets apart true leaders. That great equalizer is *values*. While each leader may have expressed it in different ways and used distinct language to describe it, the outcome was the same. True leaders define, promote and defend an organization's purpose through its values.

Dan Price, CEO of Gravity Payments said it most simply: "You have to be so passionate about your values, and they have to be the number one thing people can trust you on." Similarly, Ted Baseler of Ste. Michelle Wine Estates said, "Integrity, trust and respect are the values that create a culture's foundation."

VALUES DRIVE VALUE

Companies face new leadership challenges. Those challenges include developing Millennials and multiple generations of leaders; meeting demand for leaders with global fluency and flexibility; building the ability to innovate; inspiring others to perform; and acquiring new levels of understanding of rapidly changing technologies and new disciplines and fields.[1] That said, it makes sense that values define what a company is and wants to be. And yet, so many leaders stumble over this defining step and ultimately tumble the organization into oblivion. When the values are clear and firm, they inform decisions at all levels. But as we'll see, that's just the beginning. In their own words, here's how a few leaders most explicitly view values as the fundamental root system of their organization.

Josh Dirks, Project Bionic:

Leadership is about helping identify a common set of values and a core mission; then empowering employees to execute that mission while supporting and removing the roadblocks they face on a daily and weekly basis. Bottom-up management, if you will.

We achieve business results by creating 'comfortability' – a combination of accountability and comfort for customers, partners, affiliates – whomever we interact with. When there is a clear direction or objective, it ensures people's thoughts, words and actions consistently align with that goal or direction. When everyone is in agreement around those goals and values, it creates a uniform product or service that people know they can trust. It creates a long-term brand to which friends and family refer business.

Norm Rice, Seattle Foundation:

Leaders always tie the work to the values and vision of the organization. As mayor of the city of Seattle, I took the team through the visioning process to establish the values that the administration would adhere to in our work. We developed goals and charged individuals with developing the framework in which to implement those goals and live out those values. At the end of day, it's the values that drive the aspirations and goals of the organization.

In any organization, change happens and new things occur. When managers and team leaders can articulate how what they're proposing fits the values, you're usually going to have success. If they can't tie the work to those values, you have a disconnect and won't have a good outcome – nor will you develop good leaders.

Sunny Gupta, Apptio:

We think about leadership in terms of our cultural values and cultural philosophy. It's about how every employee, not just executives, behaves and acts every single day to further the cause of Apptio. It's important that every employee act like a leader because we are creating a new market and a new category.

We think about leadership as a set of core tenets, and it starts with creating wildly successful customers. Everything we do is focused on how we create wildly successful customers. Our product development has to be done with deep customer validation, as does our marketing, our Web site, etc. We approach every customer meeting with the attitude that this has to be the best possible interaction with that customer.

The second tenet is the glass is half empty. Some people think of this as negative, but it's really about taking the approach of continuous improvement. If there are 10 outcomes and eight are good and two are bad, we focus on improving the two that aren't working.

We believe that in companies like ours – probably in every company – 90% of the days aren't good. You deal with problems – whether it's a product issue or something with a customer – and the only way to build a real, long-term company is by following your leadership principles. I would say our entire business growth comes from abiding by our core tenets. So, every wildly successful customer becomes a reference for us to go sell to the next 10 customers. We deliver new products that receive significant customer validation, so we know there's a market and customers want to buy them. We want to ensure our customers want to be our references; they want to talk about us in the press.

Third, act like an owner. We want every employee to act as if they own the company, meaning they should see every dollar they spend as if it's their own money. Every dollar needs to demand a return for shareholders. Lastly, we develop people from within. People have different career and financial goals, and we want to help develop them so they can reach those goals. When people leave, we are very proud when other companies want to hire someone from Apptio. That signifies that we're doing our job.

Our focus on continuous improvement, or the glass half empty approach, has paid off. There were a couple of quarters when revenue numbers were down, and we focused like crazy on fixing what wasn't working. We could have had the perspective that the last five quarters were great – and there are so many great things happening in the company – why bother thinking about one bad quarter? But we chose not to. We chose to attack the problems head on, whether it was an issue with lead generation or increasing the effectiveness of our sales team or developing a product fix. We are capitalists, here to build value for our shareholders and deliver innovation to our customers, so the leadership principles drive our business execution and business results. That's why we stick to them so closely.

It's the same as raising kids to follow your family's values. The leadership principles at Apptio are no different. They guide our behavior as leaders and what we model to our employees.

Values Endure

Jon Bridge notes that core values are so strong they transcend your current position or even your career. "Your legacy, and the way you leave it, is critical," he says. "Whatever drives your passion is most important. I do it through my work with the Alliance for Education and Kid's Company and the Military Bar Committee. I want to leave a mark to make the world better for children and for our future. And I want my children and their children to have these values and do the same for the people they touch."

ONE VALUE, ONE FOCUS

Sometimes, rather than discussing a range of values, people spoke of a single value that is so strong it define the business.

Jon Bridge, Ben Bridge Jeweler:

Leadership means having good people working with you; people who you trust and to whom you can delegate. That allows you to do many good things in the community, and that's what makes life worthwhile.

What's different in a family business is there's a certain amount of personal pride in ownership. We treat everyone here like family, and since we believe in nepotism, unlike a lot of companies, many people here *are* family. We have a father and son who are managers at two different stores. My daughter managed a store. We have two brothers, one who manages a store in Bellevue, and his older brother is vice president of merchandising. The daughter of our vice president of sales for the Northwest stores is in our buying department. And that same vice president's nephew manages a store in Texas; her other nephew is doing a great job in store set-up.

John Oppenheimer, Columbia Hospitality:

Leadership means caring about people and knowing how to maintain the intimacy of a small firm, while growing the company – being big, but acting small. In measuring leadership, leaders are judged by what they do and how they help and develop others. The best leaders know how to start with a kernel and develop those kernels into popcorn. Our leaders help others produce results beyond their wildest dreams.

We all love to succeed. And if our leaders help others, our team members will be happy, successful individuals – which permeates throughout the company as a whole and ultimately translates to our guests.

Ray Heacox, NBC KING 5:

Cultures that are successful start with core values that people connect to emotionally. In our business, anyone who is serious about journalism has made a personal commitment to finding and telling the truth. That's their core. Some of the public may see journalists – like politicians – in a negative light, but we're the watchdogs of accountability. A journalist's job is one of the most important aspects of a free society.

Now, lots of people start with that focus. And others get into news to be on television. That's not us. That's not our culture. We are about doing the right thing, uncovering corruption, keeping people informed, making sure we provide information to help people live better lives. Our work can change laws, hold people accountable and get them fired if that's what's needed. Those are heavy responsibilities, if you take them seriously, and so it's important to lead with principle. That's a trait that must be supported above all others.

IN OTHER WORDS

As diverse as values can be, so too, is the language used to describe them. It turns out that one person's values are another's pillars or even a scoreboard. Dr. Paul Ramsey chose the word *pillars*, and within the context of what he said you'll see that the pillars he describes serve the same function as the values mentioned by Ted Baseler, Norm Rice and Sunny Gupta.

Dr. Paul Ramsey, UW Medicine:

Of the more than 24,000 employees at UW Medicine, more than 1,000 people are in significant leadership positions, and approximately 100 are in the most senior leadership roles. Our leadership focus is the single mission of improving the health of the public. UW Medicine leadership decisions are based on the principle that patients are first. Four pillars underpin the work we do to support that principle and ultimately tie it directly to our mission. They are:

- Providing the highest-quality patient care

- Providing service to patients and families

- Being the employer of choice—which means a focus on how we treat one another within UW Medicine

- Being fiscally responsible

The four pillars provide the means for assessing performance. We have had the same mission – with that single focus – since the UW Medicine Board approved the mission statement in 2000. We attempt to make our decisions in support of the mission to improve health. The UW Medicine mission fits very well with the national healthcare reform goals of improved healthcare for individuals, better health for the population and reduction and control of healthcare costs – the 'triple aim'. We cannot succeed with our mission unless we control costs and improve care, service and access.

We evaluate UW Medicine leadership based on their individual role with the four pillar goals. Depending on the individual's leadership role, annual strategic goals and objectives are used to track performance. We use dashboards to evaluate progress and performance on a frequent basis.

Teresita Batayola, International Community Health Services (ICHS):

At ICHS, there are formal and informal leadership roles. We have healthcare professionals – such as doctors, dentists, nurses – who are naturally perceived as leaders because of their jobs, though they do not hold formal leadership titles. Community leaders also help drive our mission. They are informal leaders because of their impact and effect, not because of their position within ICHS. Because we're community based, there is tremendous value in those informal roles.

At ICHS, leadership is about how we provide affordable, high-quality care to those who need it. A few years ago, during our management leadership retreat, we felt we had to rejuvenate the organization – especially during the recession when we kept losing funding. We re-developed our strategic plan to focus on being sustainable as a business and creating new business lines while shelving initiatives that were no longer moving us forward. We looked ahead and repositioned ourselves with a new plan for the future.

The management team is charged with moving the strategic plan forward, and we have deliverables and performance measures tied to it. We set goals and benchmark against other healthcare providers that are similar to us both statewide and on a national scale. We monitor our progress closely and make course corrections regularly.

We use a performance scorecard at the organizational level that tracks our performance in ICHSQ: infrastructure, customer service, human investment, sustainability and quality. These are the five components that directly tie to our mission and are our quantitative measures for results. For example, we can't succeed organizationally if our customer service isn't open, adjustable and flexible for meeting a person's needs. Results flow up by each department, and each director or manager owns measurements. That accountability is the way we tie leadership directly to the impact for the organization.

Relearn the Values We Learned Growing Up

And circling back to Gravity Payments' CEO Dan Price, who provides a solid final thought on values:

#CEOpov

There are really good things we know intuitively, or are taught growing up, and they are in conflict with most business philosophies. In business, we unlearn the good things we're raised with — caring for other people, treating people how you want to be treated and leaving a legacy — leaving behind something that you're really proud of. Business often teaches us to brush your own conscience aside and push things under the rug. One of the key tenets of the financial service industry is to make things complicated and opaque. We want to be the opposite of that. While we see it, and are sometimes victims of it, we want to create a lasting change.

VALUES AREN'T ENOUGH

As vital as values are, for leaders to be stewards of an organization's vision and purpose, they aren't enough. Leaders must also have the competencies to run their organizations. Because values vary from one organization to another, so too, do the competencies needed to support them. Still, certain common ground appeared and reappeared throughout my conversations.

To organize the information gleaned from those interviewed, I've borrowed *The Leadership Challenge* framework[2] developed by experts Jim Kouzes and Barry Posner and presented in their book of the same title. This framework helps logically organize the opinions of this eclectic group of leaders. Kouzes' and Posner's study of personal-best leadership shows the similar paths taken by people who guide others along pioneering journeys. Those paths are marked by five common patterns of practice. They are:

1.   Model the way

2.   Inspire a shared vision

3.   Challenge the process

4.   Enable others to act

5.   Encourage the heart

By no means should what follows be thought of as a recap or synopsis of the great work of these researchers. Its purpose here is merely to serve as a brief and simple framework for organization. And in looking at competencies, it's important to keep in mind that they don't stand alone. Leading organizations develop competencies to directly support their values. That's evident in how specific the competencies described are, even within the broad frameworks defined by Kouzes and Posner.

It's also important to keep in mind that none of the leaders I interviewed is limited to a single competency. They all exhibit skills in all these areas. I've chosen to organize their responses in this way simply because some of their comments particularly stood out during our conversations.

Model the Way

Some leaders establish principles concerning the way people should be treated and the way goals should be pursued. Titles are granted, but your behavior is what wins you respect. Exemplary leaders know that if they want to gain commitment and achieve the highest standards, they must be models of the behavior they expect of others.

Here are insights from leaders who truly model by example: Ted Baseler, John Rubino and Greg Rankich.

Ted Baseler, Ste. Michelle Wine Estates:

You can't talk about how important leading is; you have to show its importance by example. Leadership correlates with sustained business results, by understanding what's big and what's insignificant. One of my favorite sayings is, 'Excellence is the management of impact issues.' People get bogged down in the unimportant tasks and lose focus on the important priorities. Maybe it's because they're perfectionists, but they end up micro-managing issues that don't matter.

When the wrong issues are the focus, the right resources aren't allocated. Whether it's the sale of the company or the layout of the parking lot, leaders need to empower their team to make decisions. The best way is to communicate the impact issues and to support the team in finding solutions. A hallmark of our leaders is understanding where we are as a business and rallying the team around the big issues, not the little stuff – the minutia – that gets in the way. According to a national survey of corporate America, Ste. Michelle Wine Estate employees rank in the top 1% for engagement. That's a big deal.

John Rubino, GreenRubino:

We like to empower people who think outside the box; who have those leadership skills and qualities. We're small, nimble and growing. When you're new to our company, it's difficult to say, 'Here's your progression path.' That's because we make it easy to take on added responsibility. Once you've demonstrated you can handle it, and you ask for more, we're the first to give it. It doesn't matter what level you are or what title you have.

There's the traditional definition of business results that looks at revenue growth and profitability. But there are also the intangibles like client satisfaction: when a client compliments us on a job well done, or an employee who's taking a client's business to the next level, or the relationship a client has with someone on our staff. Those softer results are equally important. When people feel empowered in our organization and experience our growth, they can find success at every level. That's what drives loyalty, which is a key metric for us. We want our people to stick around.

Greg Rankich, Xtreme Consulting Group, Inc.:

When you're an owner, you have to separate ownership and leadership. Some owners have the mentality of, 'You have to listen to me because I pay your salary.' Here, leadership is about creating a great culture for managing people, managing expectations, setting goals, motivating people and making sure it's a fun environment to work in. I think sometimes people forget I'm the owner, and that's what I strive for.

My leadership style is best described using the famous General George Patton quote: 'If you tell people where to go, but not how to get there, you'll be amazed at the results.' I help people set expectations with a clear goal in mind. I provide guidance if they need it, but let them get there on their own.

Inspiring a Shared Vision

Some Leaders passionately believe that they can make a difference. They see the future, and create an ideal and unique vision of what the organization can become. Through their magnetism and quiet persuasion, these leaders enlist others in their vision and get people to see exciting possibilities for the future. Beth Wojick, Scott Oki, Norm Rice and Brad Tilden are passionate leaders who look for that same level of passion in others:

Beth Wojick, Special Olympics:

What does leadership mean at Special Olympics? It's a broad question, because leadership reaches all aspects of the organization. We have 8,000 volunteers and 10,000 athletes, so not only is our staff required to lead, but we count on our coaches and board of directors, too. Everyone here has a leadership role.

My position is constantly measured against the business. People will tell you it's lonely at the top… I don't buy into that thinking. I say it's as challenging as you want to make it. I'm a change agent; always have been. I push hard. I recognize that because of this, I actually make my job harder for myself. Sometimes I do ask myself, 'What are you doing?' Then I recognize the power of the future.

Scott Oki, Oki Developments:

Trusting who you put in charge is real leadership. I spend less than 1% of my time on our businesses. Nancy Cho was my CFO. When we started developing, buying and investing in businesses – golf courses, Nishino Japanese restaurant and the Nanny & Webster baby blanket business – I turned everything over to Nancy. She became COO and president, and that lead to her being promoted to CEO. I trust her judgment on virtually everything. That's leadership.

Positive, sustained business results goes hand-in-hand with committed, long-term leadership. I firmly believe that short term, revolving door leadership will almost never result in long-term success. Nancy has been with me for almost 20 years and her commitment and tenure mirror that of her team.

Norm Rice, Seattle Foundation:

I look at leadership as the ability to synthesize ideas, put them into action, and motivate those who need to achieve those goals to be successful. One of the most important things about leadership is developing measurable goals and metrics. Taking the leadership team through that exercise allows you to put in place the indicators that help measure success. It's the leader working with his or her colleagues to develop that structure.

Brad Tilden, Alaska Airlines:

During the last decade, there was a time when 70% of the seats flying around the country were on bankrupt airlines. As a leader in the airline industry, you have to ask yourself, 'Why was that?' I don't know if it was bad strategy, bad execution, bad decisions, bad relationships with unions, or what. But, in the end, it all comes down to leadership. It's about the people you choose, the roles you put them in, the plan you develop, and the execution. Execution is really important for airlines, so leaders need to align and inspire their teams.

In any business, you have to produce results, and that requires strong leaders. You need to have a sustainable strategy to make sure the business works long term for all of its constituents. It needs to produce returns for investors who are financing you with billions of dollars of capital. It needs to work for customers. Customers want a service they value for a price they think is fair, because we need to keep them coming back so we can grow the business. It has to work for employees because they have to keep the airline operating safely and reliably and keep providing that service customers want. It needs to work for the communities we serve and for the environment. For our business to survive over the longer term, we need a plan that addresses all of these needs and constituents.

Challenging the Process

Some leaders search for opportunities to change the status quo. They look for innovative ways to improve the organization. They experiment and take risks, knowing that mistakes get made and accept those inevitable disappointments as learning opportunities.

Dan Levitan is a leader who has challenged process all the way to the structure of the organization.

Dan Levitan, Maveron:

I think a lot of venture firms have fallen prey to a headquarters-with-branch-offices structure, which creates silos and dysfunctional behavior. It creates some sort of sub-optimal, psychological contract – where branch offices feel inferior.

One thing that's important to us is that we think of ourselves as one firm with two offices. We are proactive in the tone we create, and consciously try to make sure that each of our three teams – investments, admin and finance – is run with a one-firm, two-offices approach. The challenge is maintaining one culture in multiple offices. In my mind, the only way you do that is by having the leader be present in those offices, and having the people in those offices understand and reinforce the culture. It's peer-to-peer influence and it's powerful.

In 2000, I had the privilege of sitting down with one of my mentors, Coach K from Duke University. He described a powerful leadership paradigm. It's a horizontal approach where the players reinforce the coach, rather than top down. I remember an interesting story about a freshman at Duke, who was wearing a jersey from the school where his cousin went. He was in the weight room with the other Duke players, and one of them asked why he was wearing that jersey. He said that he was proud of his cousin for getting into that school. The response from the players was: 'This is Duke basketball. We wear Duke.' The point is, the impact is 10 times greater coming from the players than coming from the coach.

I think there are two types of organization. Some organizations focus on outcomes and other organizations focus on process.

People get lucky and good things happen. But the difference between being lucky and being a leader of a really good business is creating a sustained period where good things happen continuously. The job of the leader is to use each success as a building block to create more. This creates a process-oriented culture. I think great organizations are focused on a process that has near-term destinations, and a culture of continuous self-improvement and continuous drive for excellence.

The greatest challenge for really good leaders is being decisive and humanitarian. Sometimes that's not possible. You read books about people like Steve Jobs and Jeff Bezos that call them terrific leaders, but they have done harsh things. Organizations become great because people are committed to driving great results, not keeping everyone happy. Leadership is not a popularity contest.

Enabling Others to Act

Some leaders foster collaboration and build spirited teams. They actively involve others. Leaders understand that mutual respect is what sustains extraordinary efforts; they strive to create an atmosphere of trust and human dignity. Father Stephen Sundborg, Phyllis Campbell, Maud Daudon and Ray Heacox are leaders who make each person feel capable and powerful.

Father Stephen Sundborg, Seattle University:

We have a highly complex set of constituents, including faculty, professional staff, other staff, administration and eight schools with varying degrees of autonomy. Leadership means having the commitment to mission and the competence to execute. Measuring leadership is complex and is based on how each part of the university moves forward in a coordinated way in relationship to the mission.

Observers who evaluate us find an extraordinarily high level of commitment to mission. And when we evaluate performance, we ask people to tell us how what they're doing ties to furthering the mission. It could be in academics, in service to the community, in the growth and development of students, in using superb technology and infrastructure. There are lots of ways to bring the mission forward, and there must always be a connection to how your leadership contributes to furthering the mission.

We are an accredited university, which means we have delineated outcomes evaluated by the accrediting body. The measurements are integrated throughout the university, not just in terms of student outcomes. For example, there are measurements for enrollment services, and tech services, residence life and academics.

Phyllis Campbell, JP Morgan Chase:

When JP Morgan Chase took over Washington Mutual in 2008, it embraced the local ties Washington Mutual had created for employees and with the community. The Northwest region of JP Morgan Chase is an 'expansion market,' meaning we're forging our way and identifying opportunities with a very entrepreneurial spirit. The result is a highly collaborative culture that spans across departments and focuses on what's fair and in the best interests of customers. In order to provide the best value and do the right thing for our customers, we have to think about them multi-dimensionally and create solutions in their best interests first; i.e., not the company's or employees' interests. Leadership means being customer-centric. We all roll up our sleeves to grow our business.

To lead a sustainable business, you have to embrace change. Jamie Dimon, chairman and CEO of JP Morgan Chase, says, 'Don't grow totals fast,' meaning don't grow for the sake of growth – don't swing for the fences. Leading and creating a sustainable business means choosing customers we trust and who trust us. It means selecting customers for the long term.

Officers are rewarded on revenue and new business, which leads toward sustainable, long-term results. It takes patience and discipline not to hit the home runs, but to create teams that build solid bases of customers. We want to find and develop leaders who think this way – do the right thing, live the values, and know how to pick customers.

In addition, we have to meet the challenges from regulators, who control and determine how we do business. We have to adapt and answer to their compliance agenda, which is evolving. Our leaders must keep this top of mind. Times are different today. We are not in a low-hanging fruit environment. We have to make sure we dot our *I*s and cross our *T*s and embrace change.

Maud Daudon, Seattle Metropolitan Chamber of Commerce:

At the Chamber, on-the-job leadership development happens through our constant interaction with civic leaders and the frequency with which we are navigating sink-or-swim situations.

We run at a rapid-fire pace, juggling multiple priorities. Because we are a very team-based organization, it's important we have clear direction with good communication. We collaborate and do a lot of brainstorming to create our annual plan each year, and each quarter we hold ourselves accountable to measure progress against the plan. Here, leadership happens at all levels. Our people are very motivated and take great initiative. Of all the teams I've had the pleasure of working with in my career, this is the most energized and capable. And because we're a small group running fast, there's a lot of interaction, which makes for deep connection to each other. Through this model of clear objectives, teamwork and collaboration, we have been successful at accomplishing the majority of our goals.

Ray Heacox, President & General Manager, NBC KING 5:

In the broadcast business, there are powerful personalities. Leading these personalities takes conflict-resolution skills and the use of competition to enhance an outcome without it creating a damaging environment. That's a tough balance to strike in such a dynamic organization that produces at least 17 hours of live content daily. In the digital age, the expectation for immediate turnaround puts people under lot of pressure to perform in very, very short time periods.

You can't be more in the moment than with news; our business is being challenged by that immediacy. We're not just TV anymore – we're TV, cable, our Web site, Facebook, LinkedIn. We measure 'likes' and track engagement. It's all about what's happening right this second, and yet we have to think long-term to run a good business. Despite the fact that the moment can be overwhelming, the hardest part is to get people focused on long-term, strategic thinking and process improvements, so we make sure we work toward the future and not just for the next moment.

Given the type of business we're in, our leadership is instrumental to our success. We have an eclectic team of people with different styles and strengths and weaknesses, and it's often difficult to get all the parts to work well together – yet it's critical to our mission. The everyday leadership at KING is collaborative and collective. For example, in news, the top leaders review scripts every day. They work with reporters to help them become even better storytellers because our whole organization needs to be really good storytellers. We have rank, but we all have brains and we work together to find the best solutions.

When there's breaking news, however, a certain few people must be 'take-the-hill' leaders. There must be a captain, typically the news director, who provides orders to lieutenants. By the very nature of breaking news, each event requires a different response. If it's an earthquake, or a shooting in downtown, the leader must mobilize the right people (reporters, photographers) and the logistics (helicopters, trucks). In the moment, they need to determine the real story and what's behind it and react immediately. The news director owns it and has to be clear on all those moving parts. They have to trust their team to do their job, but they must know what they're entrusting them to do. They can't afford to let others make mistakes. Mistakes can be costly to the people we serve or our ratings, so you have to have leaders who are maniacal about taking the hill. They have to be demanding, in a classic, top-down style, because when things go wrong, that one person is responsible. Generally, as a company, our style is collaborative. But when it's time to take the hill, and if you're not ready, get out of the way.

In a typical business world, it's sacrilegious not to start with results. What's the win? What's the right analysis? And while that's important in terms of leadership, we don't back into results. We create an environment where sometimes we break glass to make glass. Because of the nature of our environment, mistakes get made. So it's important to have the right strategy in place with a clear goal and everyone's buy-in. Then, the right team of people with the right tools can own it and the output will speak for itself.

Encouraging the Heart

Accomplishing extraordinary things in organizations is hard work. Leaders show appreciation and recognize people's contributions. Encouragement can come from dramatic gestures or simple actions, through individual recognition and group celebrations. Dan

Price, Pamela Hinckley and Jon Bridge encourage the heart in different ways, but they all focus on people first.

Dan Price, Gravity Payments:

Leadership is about vision – seeing where we're trying to go and staying focused on that. We lead to that vision while staying true to who we are and what makes us who we are. In our industry, we're really trying to help independent businesses and, in general, stick up for the little guy. Most in our industry accelerate their growth and their vision by doing the opposite – taking advantage of independent business owners, or not taking them into consideration. That's really at the core of our leadership and why we do what we do. If we had a lot of success without staying true to our core, it wouldn't really be worth anything.

We do things in a certain way. We like to be very progressive and push really hard. It's not a tame environment, which we're okay with. We like to be really creative and outsmart and outthink our competition, be it actual competition or just competing against ourselves.

We really value honesty, transparency and simplicity and try to make sure that at every stage of our development, we become *more* transparent and *more* elegant, rather than making things more complicated.

From a leadership standpoint, the most important thing to me is seeing each person as a unique human being. Business results have to do with numbers. They are at odds because when business results are measured by numbers, by definition, you're not seeing people as people anymore. And so we try to synthesize those aspects when we can, but sometimes we have to balance them. I think the two key factors that you balance are seeing every individual as an individual and then also seeing the team as a collective.

Sometimes we've had really great business results, but not really taken care of people in a way that we would be proud of. Other times, we've done a great job taking care of people, but that was not reflected in the business results we achieved. Both have to be in line with the vision, because that's what funds all the good stuff.

Pamela Hinckley, Tom Douglas Restaurants:

Leadership means inspiring the team to grasp Tom's passionate vision of hospitality. That means keeping the whole group focused on excellent customer service and food quality. In this business, there is a lot of rote day-to-day operational work that needs to get done to keep the restaurants running, but what fires people up is finding new and fresh ways to think about our guests, and our partners, and how to be increasingly competitive in this crazy, busy food town called Seattle.

Recently, we had a wonderful conversation about this in our general manager's meeting. Investing in and taking care of our people drives business sustainability. Tom always wants to be the best place to work in town. Typically, kitchen workers are paid barely above minimum wage. We developed a merit system and pay based on the value of those individual's contribution. Further, we go beyond taking care of people from a financial standpoint, by ensuring people are healthy in a spiritual and emotional way. And, of course, making sure everyone is well fed.

As soon as Tom had a dime to his name, he made sure employees were insured. Last year, we introduced a wellness challenge for the entire company. While it was slow to get off the ground, we've seen it gain momentum and cause a big stir. Now, we've made it an annual program. For example, March is meditation month and we'll all meditate together. Companywide, we're doing the 'Bon Appétit – Food Lovers Cleanse.' It requires cooking very high-end food, spectacular ingredients, which I think will keep everyone's interest. It's not just drinkin' lemon water.

We also made an enormous effort to bring people out to our farm in Prosser, Washington, which really cemented relationships. It's powerful when you work together in the field, spend the night cooking together – and then go back to the restaurant and the food you helped grow gets delivered to the restaurants.

Our commitment to these efforts keeps turnover low in a traditionally high-turnover industry. I think people find comfort in the resources we provide. We try to nurture and grow people, and while they may leave to experience another aspect of hospitality or work for another restaurant group, they often find their way back to us. We have an impressive rehiring record.

We also try to develop our leaders from within by creating an inspiring environment of opportunity. Every general manager in each of the restaurants started as a server. Only on rare occasions have we had to look out-of-house for specific leadership expertise, like finance. Generally, we grow our own, and we want our team to understand that the way we're doing something isn't necessarily the way it has to be done. We want suggestions on how to improve things.

We've seen how amazing and powerful it is when employees take responsibility for creating something. There's a great sense of pride in galvanizing their efforts. For example, we have a server at the Dahlia Lounge who loves scotch and asked if we could do a high-end scotch tasting and Scottish dinner. We love that idea and we're excited to do it.

Jon Bridge, Ben Bridge Jeweler:

My background is in law, and I teach military law in ROTC. My favorite part to teach is leadership. One way to avoid legal problems is by showing true leadership and caring about people.

Leadership means having good people working with you; people who you trust and who you can delegate to. Measuring leadership is about the team being on the same bus. You have a strategy, goals and objectives that the executive team has collaborated on and established. Ed [co-CEO and president] and I may be the drivers, but everyone in the company has agreed to get on the same bus and go to the same place.

For a retail company, longevity is a measure of leadership. We have an incredible record of longevity, and nearly all our managers have come up through the ranks. At the same time, we know there's risk in being too ingrown. So, while we favor promoting from within, we also try to keep open channels to the outside world and bring in new blood when we find it.

Prepare for the Future

These conversations show that leading companies have successfully navigated the complex geography of core values and the competencies that support those values. And yet as rare as that success is, it's not enough: These companies must navigate that terrain again and again as they prepare for the future by developing leaders who can emulate that success. They share how they do that in the next chapter.

Now, take a second to think about how you define your own values. How do they align with your leadership and those values of the broader organization at all levels.

IN YOUR OWN WORDS

1.   Which one or two core values define who you are?

_____

_____

_____

2.   How do you express and reinforce those values at work? (In other words, how do people know what your values are? If they don't know, why not?)

_____

_____

_____

3.   How are your values integrated into the organization? (Consider how the organization recruits and hires, what the organization rewards, and so on.)

_____

_____

_____

4.   How do you ensure employees drive decisions based on those values?

_____

_____

_____

5.   What do you need to stop doing to ensure you're living your values?

_____

_____

_____

PART 4: FROM THEIR PERSPECTIVE: IDENTIFYING FUTURE LEADERS

RESEARCH TELLS US

Undoubtedly, the best and truest leaders search for significance in their work. And there is nothing more significant then developing the leaders of the future. But finding those leaders is no small task.

Before the 2007-2009 recession, most companies were cruising on auto-pilot, hiring who they wanted, when they wanted, where they wanted. However, when a recession hits, history repeats itself. According to research, high unemployment rates across the U.S. and abroad did not create the talent surplus many would have predicted.[1] Now, we're shifting from the recession to growth, and many executives predict further talent shortages across key business units (such as research and development and executive leadership) that are needed to drive innovation and growth. A quick read between the lines of the many comments I heard revealed that finding this top talent, developing it, and keeping it are pressing topics around the table of every boardroom.

As we emerge from the ashes and look forward, research shows that future-focused companies and leaders are hitting *rethink* instead of *reset*. What worked before will not work now, or in the future.

The results from Deloitte's *Talent Edge 2020 Survey Series* help illustrate where we ended up in the arena of leadership talent, and whether the road ahead is paved with yellow bricks or asteroid-size potholes.

Deloitte and *Forbes Insights* polled senior business leaders and talent managers at large companies worldwide across a range of major industries on changing talent priorities and strategies. This survey, *Blueprints for the New Normal,* is the first in the series, post-recession. The research revealed that focusing on developing leaders and succession planning is a high priority. Below is a combination of the key findings from the section of that survey called "Creating the Next Generation of Leaders" and the latest research on global human capital trends. Of the CEOs surveyed worldwide:

- 56% forecast leadership shortages, and developing the next generation of corporate leaders is seen as a clear imperative among senior executives.[2]

  - Leadership remains the number one talent issue facing organizations around the world, with 86% of respondents in the survey rating it "urgent" or "important"[3]

  - 66% believe they are "weak in their ability to develop Millennial leaders."[4]

- 38% said developing leaders and succession planning is the second most pressing talent concern. The first is competing for talent globally and in emerging markets.[5]

  - 38% of all respondents rated building global leadership as by far the most urgent (Yes, ironically it is the same number as above). Companies see the need for leadership at all levels, in all geographies, and across all functional areas.[6]

- Three years from now, executives predicted leadership development would be their greatest talent concern.

  - In a world where knowledge doubles every year and skills have a half-life of two and a half to five years, leaders need constant developing.

  - This ongoing need to develop leaders is also driven by the changing expectations of the workforce and the evolving challenges businesses are facing, including two major themes underlying this year's trends: globalization and the speed and extent of technological change and innovation.[7]

As the global workforce continues to age, and the massive Baby Boomer generation begins to retire, executives and talent managers are deploying a variety of strategies to fill the leadership pipeline at their companies. Not only are companies not developing enough leaders, but they are also not equipping the leaders they are building with the critical capabilities and skills they need to succeed. A premium is placed on speed, flexibility, and the ability to lead in uncertain situations.

How are executives zeroing in on the right talent to train and develop into future leaders? According to *Blueprints for the New Normal*:

- More than seven out of 10 (71%) executives expect to increase the focus on developing high-potential employees and emerging leaders.

- A similar percentage (69%) reported they plan to increase recruitment efforts for experienced hires.

- 72% are increasing their focus on fundamental workforce planning tools, such as performance management.

- Many companies are also engaged in efforts to fast-track the development of new corporate leaders: 64% of the survey participants plan to increase their focus on accelerated leadership programs.

In addition, executives see higher turnover among key talent segments and know they need new strategies to retain key employees:

- More than six in ten (64%) have a high (40%) or very high (24%) fear of losing high-potential talent and leadership.

- 60% have a high (35%) or very high (25%) level of concern about turnover among top managers and other executive leadership.

Moving forward, participants are taking clear actions to place a greater emphasis on leadership. Although all executives plan to increase their focus on emerging and senior leaders, firms with retention plans are more focused on these issues than their counterparts without plans. More than eight in ten (81%) companies with retention plans are increasing their focus on emerging leaders (vs. 62% without plans) and 78% of firms with plans in place are strengthening senior leadership priorities (vs. 53%).

High-potential Millennial leaders want to be identified early and want their development accelerated. Mid-career leaders want challenging roles that allow them to make leaps that deepen and broaden their leadership skills to prepare them for more senior roles.[8]

When asked which retention initiatives would be most effective in appealing to Millennials, non-financial incentives topped the list, led by company culture (21%), flexible work arrangements (20%), new training programs (19%), and support and recognition from supervisors or managers (19%). Additional compensation was ranked 14th out of 15, and "additional bonuses or financial incentives" was ranked 11th out of 15.

FAVORITISM. YOU SAY IT LIKE IT'S A BAD THING

Although emerging leaders' motivations are different, the leadership characteristics used to identify them have not changed. Those characteristics sought by leaders are unique to each company and to each leader's point of view, but leaders were unanimous in their answers regarding two specific aspects:

- In every leader's head, there is an unspoken list of people who they consider the 'rock stars,' high-potentials in their company – the ones they want to invest in and keep.

- And every leader agreed that when they focus on the rock stars there's always a risk of showing favoritism, but there are ways to manage that perception.

The second point was curious to me. I wondered if some of these leaders were just being polite. In my humble opinion, good leaders *should* favor those employees who merit it. Although you don't outwardly admit you favor one child over another, when the oxygen mask drops from above the truth becomes obvious. Similarly, workplace favoritism is a sensitive issue, but the same principle applies: Time and wisdom are precious, so leaders need to pick wisely with whom they share it. The ones with the highest potential deserve the generosity of a leader's time, insight, feedback and wisdom.

That said, here is a variety of commentary on the characteristics leaders look for in those deemed future leaders, favoritism, time spent one-on-one, and how the company as a whole develops its star performers. As in previous chapters, we'll look at this issue through the framework developed by Kouzes and Posner.

Model the Way

TED BASELER, STE. MICHELLE WINE ESTATES
Translating Energy Into Motivation

We want people who have positive energy and an optimistic out-look. Great leaders are positive and demanding. Negativity and political aspirations don't win popularity contests and probably won't get you past go at Ste. Michelle Wine Estates. Leaders don't have to be charismatic, but they have to have an energy that translates into motivation for others, and shows a constant demonstration of integrity, trust and respect.

There's an important connection between motivating teams to get amazing results and positive energy.

On my list of high-potentials are candidates who demonstrate a keen understanding of what their job requires, and who have the capabilities to perform at a higher level.

Those leaders come in from the different business units and have the opportunity to present to me. I respectfully challenge their thinking to uncover whether they have true conviction or if it's just superficial.

Favoritism is inevitable. You see it by who gets promoted in America – and in the greater business world. However, when performance shows quantifiable progress then there's greater clarity in other areas.

Every year, two- to three- dozen employees gather at Chateau Ste. Michelle for its annual executive leadership forum. Employees are selected to attend based on their position and their role as a leader. Often, employees are selected because they've been identified as an up-and-comer – a person who has the potential for higher advancement in the company.

The two-day event includes a 360-degree assessment and training. This is a winery, so some of that training includes product testing. No one seems to mind that. One of the pinnacle moments of the training is when everyone is presented with the case study of Ernest Shackleton's failed quest to reach the South Pole more than 100 years ago.

The teams examine the dynamics of the crew, as they waited on the ship, stranded by an ice floe. Shack tells the crew, inaccurately, that they're required to stay on the ship. He lied to save their lives, and it shows a certain quality of thinking. It's the cornerstone of our training.

Someone who has the aptitude for a higher level of leadership gets the additional training they need to help them get there. Every employee receives a regular performance evaluation that tries to align the person's aspirations to the company's goals. That gives people a pretty clear sense as to where they should expect to end up. The key is good, honest dialogue – done respectfully. This is what can motivate people to higher levels.

JOHN RUBINO, GREENRUBINO
Boiling It Down to Initiative

When I look for someone to mentor, I look for someone who thinks outside of his or her job description. I look for someone who asks a lot of questions, and who goes beyond what I ask them to do. Or they do something in a way I didn't even think about, and it turns out better than I would have done. That boils down to initiative. I give them more responsibility and earmark them as an up-and-comer.

My partner, Cam Green, and I have separate lists of high potentials in our head. When we discuss them, there tends to be some overlap and it's interesting when we see things differently. Sometimes it takes one of us longer to see the potential in individuals on the other person's list, and it's fun to have those conversations.

It's my responsibility to create a culture that breeds leadership behavior, one that's open to ideas rather than one that squashes innovation. Personally, I am open to paying back. I want to do what Peter Harleman, my mentor, did for me. In the nine years I've been with GreenRubino, I've mentored a number of people.

I try to avoid favoritism, because in a smaller company, you have to be cognizant of perceptions. However, as a leader, you want to spend more time supporting, developing, and encouraging those employees who show initiative and their potential as future leaders.

Our goal is to hire people with high potential across the board, because leadership can come from anywhere. We have gotten very good at recruiting and screening and developing at every level.

We abandoned the performance evaluation model because it was ineffective and laborious and it never was a true reflection of an employee's performance or capabilities, especially when done only once in a rush at the end of each year. We use more of a one-on-one coaching model. We meet with individuals more frequently, but less formally. We capture key components of the conversation and document and file them. It's a simple process that helps mold people's performance. We compliment what they did well, and course-correct where needed. It's done in real time and fosters the development of an employee, instead of focusing on performance for a raise.

We also make sure we have fun. We've instituted GR8, the GreenRubino Great Rewards, which encourages team members to compliment each other. Pats on the back don't have to come from the leader. At our Great Day monthly breakfast, employees fill out GR8 Awards. It might be for a job well done on a difficult project, or staying late because a proposal was due. Every month at the agency meeting one GR8 form gets pulled from a hat and the winner receives a gift certificate. Then everyone gets the GR8 awards that were written to him or her. That way recognition happens on every level.

GREG RANKICH, XTREME CONSULTING
Being 1000% Pro-Company

I'm driven by helping other people grow. I look for people who want to be successful and make everyone around them successful. I watch how they interact with people – through words, through actions, through their own personal growth. I look for potential leaders who ask, 'How do I grow the team underneath me?' We do a lot to keep company morale high and try to make people feel this is a family more than a business. When I was at Microsoft, I was 1000% pro-company, and everything I did was with that mindset. I didn't think about myself or where I was going. I look for people who are willing to jump in to make the company better even if it's not in their job description. Those are the people I want to invest in and have as leaders in my company.

I know who my replacement is. I'm only 41 and not ready to step aside, but we both know who he is. He's working on his own growth to fill in the gaps, so he can be that leader when the time is right.

I have bi-monthly, skip-level meetings with a few specific people. They don't have direct responsibility to me, but I see them as future leaders in the company and make sure I set aside time to give them feedback and discuss their progress. Most people know me well enough to know I'm supportive of everyone and try to jump in and help everyone all the time. It's also important to me to treat people like family and really know them as people. It helps you recognize and understand their goals. Some people don't want to be managers, and others clearly want to move up. I'm constantly trying to think of how I can help people move forward on either path.

If someone perceives favoritism, they probably don't recognize the values of our culture. I always joke with one guy here. He came to work with us straight out of college and has been here almost four years. He started as a temporary receptionist and now runs accounts receivable for one of our major clients. I always tell him he's so spoiled here. If he ever leaves, it's going to feel like a hard slap across the face, because he'll realize how good he had it here. We do a lot for a lot of people and try not to create that inner circle.

As part of our review process, people list their annual educational goals. I'm a big believer in education and continuous learning. I help my team set stretch goals and figure out how to get what they need to accomplish them. I'll pay for classes and let them take the days off. For example, last year the accounting group learned expert-level Excel. This year, they're learning SQL databases. Does every accountant here need to have this level of understanding? Probably not. But I push them into areas that aren't necessarily their job today, but long term, having that knowledge may help them in their career.

I think it' important to invest in people's future. I'm encouraging our VP of recruiting to get his MBA, which I'm happy to pay for because I think it will really help him understand the financial side of our business.

Keeping great people is my goal, but it's a challenge to keep leaders motivated when there's no career path left. I think it's important to figure out how to keep people engaged by creating a great culture, giving constructive feedback and pushing people to develop themselves. Money is the easiest answer, but it's not what drives everyone. I want to work with people who want to work for a great company, which means you have to be creative in the ways you motivate and challenge people.

Inspire a Shared Vision

BETH WOJICK, SPECIAL OLYMPICS
Playing to People's Strengths

I just had a meeting with a staff member who I see as our future. And I've seen him as our future since I started five years ago. He's a quick learner and willing to take risks, which I think is huge as part of leadership. He's got high self-esteem, inspires others – really has that type of personality. I think there's always room for the 8:30 to 5 kind of person who is the Rock of Gibraltar – the one who gets the basic work done. But that person is never going to be the one who steps up to lead.

I worked at Seafair for 16 years and was constantly around military leadership, including high-ranking officials from the U.S. Navy, Army and Coast Guard as we organized the Blue Angels' performances and Fleet Week. These seasoned leaders taught me to surround myself with five key people. If it's more than five, it's ineffective.

In my case, it's my Board chair and my four vice presidents. I try to keep it to that and not dive any deeper. I don't attend staff meetings with anyone else, or include others in my leadership meetings. Of my four direct reports, there are two who I see as future leaders – they are the potential successors to my job.

I learned from former Seahawks coach Mike Holmgren to play to people's individual strengths. Not everyone learns the same or communicates the same. And also, it is my job to teach leadership. I use learning moments with my senior staff. For example, I may have just worked through a serious issue that's top of mind, and one of them will walk in to my office. I'll take them through the process that I just went through to show them how I thought about and handled the situation. It may be way outside the scope of what they do, but I want them to see and learn.

There's one individual here, in particular, I want to show the full breadth of the CEO job because in a couple of years I see him being able to do it.

There's another individual who's really, really strong and will play a significant role in leadership here. She may take on leadership in other departments, but may not be the one who takes on the CEO role.

There are several ways we develop high-potential managers. For one, Special Olympics International conducts national meetings and some of the sessions are directed at future leaders. I've always been a strong proponent of my senior staff participating in those sessions so they can learn and achieve more. It's also helpful for them to see and appreciate the scope of my job. Special Olympics also counts on strong leaders from various programs combining their expertise to help others. Additionally, there are national committees, and national and international events where our staff can serve, learn and grow as leaders. I'm always open and supportive if staff approaches me wanting training in a certain area, even if it is not in the budget.

SCOTT OKI, OKI DEVELOPMENTS
Quantifying Passion, Commitment and Scar Tissue

I look for people who are passionate, committed and have startup scar tissue.

I look for people who are passionate about X, Y or Z. If the passion isn't there, they won't have the commitment, which is the second thing I look for. Very rarely have I been wrong. I've had a track record of hiring insanely great people, and the core ingredient for them to be a great leader or become a better leader always is how passionate they are about the industry or about what they're doing.

I founded the International Division at Microsoft. I'm American. I grew up in Seattle and only speak English. I had no international experience. So why did Bill Gates give me a million dollars to develop the international division? Probably because I asked for it. I had worked for Hewlett-Packard, and I knew that HP and other large U.S. companies followed a formula for setting up overseas: They shipped people to the foreign country to run things and live as expats. I never understood why they did that. When I set things up in Japan, Germany, France, the UK or any other country, I looked for local leaders because they knew the lay of the land. They knew the customs, they knew the culture, they knew whom else to hire, they knew how to get things done quickly. They knew what we didn't know. And it worked out amazingly well.

One of the commonalities of all my country managers was that every single one of them had startup scar tissue. They didn't have to have run a successful startup, but they had to have experienced the passion and intensity that happens in a startup. They had to know what it meant to take risks and work hard. That's the stuff that leads to good outcomes.

I co-founded a software company in San Francisco. We raised venture capital money and in two years we ran it into the ground. But the lessons I learned from that experience are still with me today. I look for people who have common sense, have street smarts and are unafraid to go against the grain.

I mentioned passion and intensity. Intensity can mean many things – there are different levels of intensity. In 1982, when I started, Microsoft was a startup. After working there for three years, I was doing a performance review with Bill. Our days were not eight-hour days. They were long, long days and I traveled internationally a lot. In fact, in 1984, I was Pan Am's number one frequent flyer, with 400,000 miles in one year. My father-in-law was a captain for Pan Am and his full-time job was to fly; I flew twice as many miles as he did that year. So, during my review, I mentioned to Bill that I hadn't taken a single day off in those three years. To that, Bill said, "So what? I haven't taken a single day off in seven years."

It puts it in perspective. Because I worked that hard and Bill worked that hard, the expectation was that we all worked hard and we needed people who worked hard. (That was a challenge in Europe, given that the work ethic was not quite as intense.) Finding that core ingredient – people who weren't afraid of hard work – paid off in spades. In four years, the international division accounted for 43% of topline revenue and more than half the profits of the company.

I certainly have in my mind the people I think are really high potential. I interact with those people, but more so in the non-profit space than in the for-profit arena. Nancy Cho is the CEO for Oki Developments. I have full trust in Nancy, so it's really a matter of management by exception. I get involved when things are insanely good or insanely bad.

I believe that if more non-profits acted and behaved like for-profit companies, we'd be better off. For-profit boards are typically small (usually a single-digit number). In the non-profit arena, you have a lot of people who really care, but they don't necessarily all belong on a board just because they write a check. If you sit on a board of 20-50 people, your inclination is to opt out because your voice won't matter much. Changing that kind of culture is like trying to push a wet string – one person isn't going to make much of a difference.

Since retiring from Microsoft, I've served on more than 100 boards and founded or co-founded exactly 20 non-profits. Recently, I have been spending the vast majority of my time with two non-profits that I had a hand in founding. The first is SeeYourImpact.org, an organization in the micro-charity space, which I co-founded with Digvijay Chauhan, another Microsoft alum. We've added SeeYourImpact.com as well and hired Brian Donaldson, a former Microsoft guy, to be our CEO. He's smart, passionate and has startup scar tissue *and* non-profit experience. Brian would say this is his dream job. The second is TheParentsUnion.org, which I believe is the missing catalyst to cause systemic U.S. public education reform to actually happen. Tom Brubaker, CEO, is yet another Microsoft alum!

There's always the risk of favoritism, of making others feel not quite as valuable. But I also think that, more often than not, people inherently know what they're good at and what they're not so good at. I've always believed that you should focus on someone's strengths. For example, at SeeYourImpact, Steve Eisner is our chief technology officer. At one time, we considered him for the CEO position, and Steve gave it serious consideration. But at the end of the day, Steve is totally passionate about writing code and developing best-of-breed product. He's not as passionate about marketing, finance, fundraising, human resources and all the other non-technical aspects of the job of a CEO.

In developing high-potential people, it really is about spending one-on-one time with them and working on various aspects that allow them to get a sense of how I think. I look for out-of-the-box thinkers. I want people who are outspoken and have opinions. I invite them to attend meetings and witness the kinds of questions I ask. It's on-the-job training in a very individual way.

FATHER STEPHEN SUNDBORG, SEATTLE UNIVERSITY
Politicking (In the Good Sense) Can't Be Learned

In a university like this, I look for people with political skills. I identify people who demonstrate the skills it takes to work well with and inspire people, articulate the vision, move objectives forward, collaborate, compromise, confront, negotiate and build consensus.

A university is highly dependent on the relationships of the institution, and those relationships can be very complex. How you work with a complex set of people to get something done and move forward is critical. I can look at a person's qualifications, but if they don't have that political sensibility, and I mean that in a positive way, it's a very difficult skill to learn; they either have it or they don't. Second, I believe strongly in steadiness or the consistency of character. People need to be able to count on who you are and how you act.

The leadership cabinet is the president, plus 11 vice presidents, and one of the vice presidents also serves as provost. Each of us has a list of people who we've identified as potential leaders, and the lists are probably similar. The people on the lists are those who *show* themselves. They attend events, they get involved. Over time, they manifest themselves and somehow rise above the rest; they find ways to stand out.

The list tends to be the people who are repeatedly being recommended and asked to serve on search committees, strategic planning task forces, major campaign groups — those kinds of things. Out of 1,400 employees, I have a top-of-line unspoken list of probably 100 people. The downside is they're the usual suspects. I've been president of the university for 17 years, and the danger is that you tend to work with the people you know best. You don't get to know the new people as well, and how potential leaders who have come to the university in the last five years get identified is different from those who have been here for the last 10-15 years.

We offer opportunities for faculty, staff and administrators on many different levels to further their development, knowledge and understanding of what a Jesuit education means. This ranges from self-selecting into a cohort like the Colleagues in Jesuit Education, which meets six times a year, to joining The Arrupe Seminar in Ignatian and Jesuit Spirituality and Education for a much deeper dive into understanding the origins of Jesuit spirituality and education. Now there is Arrupe Two for those who want to go even further and gain a substantive understanding of the Jesuit purposes.

Many on that unspoken list of 100 are in these groups. They want to further their understanding of the fundamental Jesuit purpose and seek out ways to voluntarily increase their knowledge and understanding.

If a cabinet member makes a recommendation that someone should be included on a committee, it's usually a sign of a person feeling left out, and I'll find a way to include him or her. I sometimes hear rumblings that the same people are always asked to serve on the committees. I believe people want to be asked because they want to be recognized. A university culture is made up of people who expect their status to be recognized. When I do ask, however, they usually say yes.

We do several things to develop high-potential people. There are programs like the Ignatian Colleagues Program, which is a national program offered among the 28 colleges. The program is designed to educate and inform administrators more deeply in the Jesuit tradition of higher education so they may better articulate, adapt, and advance Ignatian mission on their campuses. The cabinet selects two people in a mid-level position to attend the 18-month program. These are people in leadership roles, such as a dean or director of enrollment, director of campus ministry or head of libraries. They've been identified as having the potential to increase their impact as leaders, and through this program, participants work on teams with other people from other Jesuit universities. They really learn the skills and tools necessary to develop as leaders of a Jesuit university.

In addition, we send three to four people to attend the Association of Jesuit Colleges and Universities Leadership Seminar, an intensive, weeklong workshop. It's intended for people at a lower-level than mid-level staff and is the first step toward attending the Ignatian Colleagues Program. We also select one person to go through the formal, Executive Leadership Certificate Program in the Albers School of Business and Economics on our campus. The cohort is mostly made up of high-level corporate managers. This is another way we find leaders, develop them and move them forward. Lastly, for the past 14 years, we've invited 15 faculty and staff to go on an eight-day immersion to Nicaragua. Seattle University subsidizes this program and we select people from all areas of the university, who are very involved in the mission. This is a deep plunge and a truly amazing experience. Those who attend consistently say the experience has been the best gift they've received from Seattle University.

We do 360-degree assessments on a regular schedule for various people in leadership positions. Based on that learning, we might provide an executive coach to help people work through issues or further their leadership development.

NORM RICE, SEATTLE FOUNDATION
Knowing When To Get Out of the Way

When we're looking for future leaders, we're looking for people who:

- Motivate others to achieve goals, meaning really motivating individuals to achieve the goals themselves, rather than the leader having to do the work.

- Are open-minded and willing to listen.

- Have the wherewithal to know when to get out of the way or exit the scene and let those managers do what they need to do to achieve their goals.

I probably have five people, who fall into the category of leaders or successors, on my mental list. For those people, the first thing is to coach – to provide a perspective to help people achieve their goals. I coordinate and recognize where the intersection is between what they're doing and how it interconnects with the rest of the organization. I make sure we hear one another, that the message from the sender is complete, not one-sided or in one direction.

I don't think there's a perception of favoritism. I spend the time with the people I need to for the job they're doing. I don't do much chatting outside of that. This includes my senior vice president for finance and mission development, but also the three others who manage the community leadership group, philanthropic services and communications. All five of us get together as a team.

We don't do enough to develop our high-potential managers. Because of our size, we don't do as much training as we probably should. We also have a longevity factor, meaning the team is a seasoned group who stays. Each has an advanced degree: MBAs or MPAs. They get great training and exposure from the conferences they attend in the community foundation sector. Whether it's finance or IT, the affinity groups are very valuable.

TERESITA BATAYOLA,
INTERNATIONAL COMMUNITY HEALTH SERVICES
Walking in Others' Shoes

Empathy and asking a lot of questions are qualities I look for in potential future leaders. In addition, we look for people with the ability to believe in, see, understand and own our mission. You have to be passionate about providing affordable care to those who need it. You have to be able to walk in our patients' shoes.

We serve displaced people, refugees or immigrants who have experienced civil unrest, natural disasters, or economic instability. To be a future leader in our organization, you must have the propensity to identify and work with this population. And, you must be able to solve problems that move our organization forward.

I have identified some potential future leaders, and I try to find ways to interact with them while still being respectful of the management chain. I do it in the organization, as well as in the community. Anyone in my position is always recruiting in his or her head. I keep an eye out for the high-potentials internally and for people in the community to attract to the organization whether we have a position or not. In good economic times, you have the luxury of creating a position. Right now, even though we are in growth mode, our current positions require specific skill sets but I am constantly promoting ICHS to attract talent.

There's always a risk of favoritism. We are informal enough that I have the luxury of saying 'Hey, let's have coffee.' I want to get to know and understand their interests before I make an investment in them. Some initiate the contact and I generally give them my time at least once.

We try to develop leaders in different ways. We don't have a set budget for leadership development. We usually look at the type of training needed for staffs to do their jobs well through a variety of internal training sessions. Different leaders have the opportunities to attend specific training through state and national healthcare organizations.

My directors are aware that we need to think organizationally. I engage my direct reports to think about helping people on their team stretch and expand their skills beyond their current assignments into more general areas. I ask them to develop and track the people who take on more responsibility.

We have a patient-centered, integrated model of care that requires people to break down silos and work across departments. If a medical patient is facing overwhelming stress, our doctor or nurse connects them to our psychologist or counselor. If a dental patient shows signs of diabetes and they have not seen a doctor for the condition, our dentist will make sure that connection is made. Our work is done through intersecting teams. To that extent, we have matrix reporting wherein specific employees have a primary supervisor but established accountabilities with other leaders.

We also have opportunities to work on special, temporary assignments that fall outside people's areas of responsibility. They are voluntary, but sometimes I'll nudge certain people toward involvement. These special opportunities range from the Care Committee (which focuses on fun ICHS activities helping staffs to socialize and know each other) to the Quality Improvement Committee (which draws a staff from each department for at least a year-long rotation to learn and carry out improvement projects in their work areas), to a limited-time task force that initiated ideas on an employee incentive program. These are good, safe ways to see how different employees perform as leaders outside their job description. It is a way to see how they deal with a new assignment, how they figure it out, how they work with others from different departments, how they proactively participate in facilitating a group process, and the recommendations they come up with based on solid information and clear thinking. It's a process and a low-risk way to test them before redefining their jobs or promoting them.

DR. PAUL RAMSEY, UW MEDICINE
Embracing One Mission

Individuals who have potential to be future leaders embrace our mission of improving health and the pillar goals. Future leaders combine support for the overall mission with their own vision for their individual role and responsibilities. They also demonstrate the ability to translate that vision into strategic goals and objectives. They make a commitment to support and mentor their people and serve their unit to make it efficient and cost effective.

I try to pay considerable attention to succession planning. This list is often in my head, and I'm constantly updating it. I consider the individual's current position, their knowledge, skills and attitudes and their current performance. I try to arrange for them to have advanced responsibility in different areas and look for opportunities for them to grow within the organization.

I interact with many on that list. Given our size, there are 100 leaders with whom I interact most, and another 200-300 with whom the interactions are less frequent, and then another 1,000 or so leaders with whom the interactions are more sporadic.

When I learn of someone who is doing a great job, I'll try to meet with him or her. This approach includes people at the junior levels. In our organization, many individuals are driven to care for patients, to do research and to teach and are not necessarily interested in an administrative role. When I hear about individuals who show administrative interest and talent, I try to meet them and provide encouragement and advice. If appropriate, I will talk to their supervisor to consider expanded responsibilities for them that may advance their career.

There's certainly the risk of the perception of favoritism. One way I try to mitigate that risk is by holding monthly meetings with six to 10 randomly selected assistant professors. These are individuals who are working very hard on their clinical care, teaching or research responsibilities and may (or may not) have some interest in administration. This is my opportunity to have a personal conversation with them and explore who they are as individuals. I can develop an initial impression about their potential, and in some cases follow up with further discussions. These lunches give me the chance to hear directly from our future leaders and many of the conversations lead to some specific follow up activities.

Our large leadership team is made up of faculty (with M.D. or Ph.D. degrees) and professional staff (those who have professional training, such as attorneys, CPAs, MBAs and other professionals who are working in administrative roles). There is a spectrum of development opportunities for them, ranging from highly competitive programs where only one person is selected (e.g., some national leadership development programs) to programs in which

400 people participate by virtue of the position they hold, and everything in between.

For the last several years, we have been running an active leadership program for our top 400 leaders, who are both faculty and professional staff. The program relates to the 'patients are first' principle and the four pillar goals that I described. This program emphasizes individual responsibility, accountability, mentorship and role modeling.

All that said, learning leadership needs to occur over time. I believe that within the sphere of leadership development, short-course leadership programs are one of the least useful things for an early-stage leader. At the right stage, an intensive, well-organized leadership course can be synergistic with other approaches. But I've seen many individuals come out of the short-course leadership programs without learning useful leadership skills. A long-term commitment to continuous self-improvement is key to leadership development.

BRAD TILDEN, ALASKA AIRLINES
Emulating the Energizer Bunny

I look for people with passion — they're self-correcting. They make a choice, they run with it, and if they hit a wall, they back up and go in a different direction – sort of like the Energizer Bunny. It can't be overstated how valuable someone like that is to an organization. Of course, the person needs to have rock-solid personal values, too.

We want people who are really smart and curious about the world. We look for people who are confident enough to challenge our strategies. Can they be tweaked? Can something be improved? We want people who are humble and have a realistic sense of their own abilities. And they should appreciate other people's abilities. We want leaders who know the people they work with are trying to do the right thing and to do a good job. I think people like that are more successful.

I've been here 23 years, and I've seen a noticeable evolution of our leadership team. We have folks here now who have a collective mindset. They all want to do well individually, but they also want their colleagues to do well. Our senior leadership group is diverse — they've got different interests, backgrounds, politics and areas of expertise. But they share values and the mindset of wanting each other to succeed. It's powerful.

We're thinking about people all the time. I had a boss 15 years ago who said, 'Every day is a job interview.' When I'm sitting in meetings with people, I'm constantly thinking, 'Could this person do more? Are there other opportunities for this person? Should we be looking for ways to get this person other experiences?'

I spend time with all of my direct reports, and I think I'm mindful of those with the highest potential. A couple of years ago, I did a skip-level review. I met one-on-one with all the managing directors in the company. I got to know them, talked about work and their challenges. But that took a year, and that makes it very challenging. I also spend a lot of time with our technology and innovation groups. It's a fast-changing area that's very important for our future.

People are our most important resource, and you want to keep everyone motivated. That said, you do want to spend extra time and get to know those who show the most potential. One of the mistakes I think a lot of us make as leaders is we spend time in the problem areas instead of spending time with the people who show the most promise and ability to help the company move forward.

We've offered a variety of leadership programs for those in senior positions. Every year, we select two senior people (often at the managing director level) to go through the University of Washington's executive MBA program. We have a variety of other development programs for emerging leaders, new leaders and experienced leaders, and these range from one- or two-day programs that are regularly offered to a weeklong offsite that we do twice a year.

Something unique to the airline industry is that, with the exception of Alaska Air Group and Southwest Airlines, every legacy carrier that was around at the time of deregulation has filed for bankruptcy. We did a turn-around mid-way through the last decade (2003 to 2007) where we took a variety of actions — outsourcing work, lowering fares and reducing costs. We did this because we realized we'd be extinct if we didn't. This was not a fun time in our history.

We had a lot of low-hanging fruit, and we could make decisions around a conference room table that could enhance our profitability by $30 or $40 million each. Today, that low-hanging fruit is gone. Our thinking is our biggest benefit, and the future is going to come from having all 13,000 of us working together, and taking good care of customers. This requires a bigger emphasis on leadership, and in particular front-line leadership.

We're a highly unionized company, and we need to make sure that degree of unionization isn't hurting our esprit de corps, our understanding of where we're headed, or our alignment around the plan. I don't think it is today because we've been through a lot with our labor groups and union leadership, and I believe we trust each other. It's important that we hang on to this.

We've launched a new leadership program called 'Gear Up.' Over the next six months, we'll bring our frontline leaders in (about 1,000 people) to talk with them about the most important leadership principles that we believe are significant to our future success. Our goal is to give the whole company a common experience, a common sense of the culture we're trying to create, and a common vocabulary which we can use as we move forward.

Challenge the Process

JOSH DIRKS, PROJECT BIONIC
Choosing Common Sense Over PhDs

We look for smart people. I personally prefer a ton of common sense over degrees and PhDs, because we're in a space where we humanize brands. I want people who are people-people first. That means they're excellent communicators, whether that's written or in person. I also look for people who are adventurous, who are willing to push boundaries. I never want people to rest on their laurels about what we achieved yesterday.

From a bottom-up level, we look for people who mirror our values as a company. Someone can do great work, but if they don't align with our values, it's not a fit. One of our values is humble leadership, so we look for people who are naturally humble in the way they present data or develop creative solutions for customers. We look for excellent performance that's done from a place of humility, rather than a place of boastfulness.

You're always evaluating your staff and identifying best and worst employees. Thinking back to my previous experience in leadership, we always looked at the Two-Thirds, One-Third Rule: Two-thirds of employees will be performers, one-third will be below that line. With that one-third, you're constantly choosing to build them, grow them or cut them loose and replace them. By managing the bottom employees and helping them excel, you continue to push what your average or top performers do because the bar is constantly being raised.

Future leaders are brought into advanced leadership sessions and advanced creative sessions. We might ask them to participate in mission and company planning sessions. They're brought in as needed, but I also just try to get lunch with them. I try to get as much personal interaction with them so I can clearly understand their vision and goals for their lives. That way, I can make sure those are in alignment with what we're doing here at the company – or that we're challenging them in those areas so they continue to see personal growth. Employees, who see personal growth aligned with their own vision for themselves, are some of the best employees because they don't feel like they're working anymore. They're doing something they love and care about.

There is a risk of perceived favoritism if you identify potential leaders in an ambiguous way. If you don't set the standards before you start the process, then it will look like favoritism. If you define what performance looks like for a future leader in your organization, and communicate that, you develop a cultural understanding. If you set measurable goals and activities around that definition within the workplace, then it's clear that those high-potentials have earned their way into that circle.

The first thing we do to develop high-potential managers is to start giving more responsibility to them by allowing them to identify areas in which we can get better in our product. Then we layer on more opportunities for strategic responsibility. We empower them to build strategy, ideas and theory that are then executed and rolled out across the entire team and measured. This is the first place they get to seriously put their own stamp on the product and really make the product their own.

Once we see consistently great performance from them, we up the ante and start to allow them to build and lead employee groups. It might be a team in another section of the company that they work with, or we start to bring them into creative sessions or planning meetings around the company itself.

Externally, we've supported several employees through mentorship, leadership classes or programs or through peer groups. We'll pay for our people to go through those courses to get the experience that rounds them out. Going back to what their personal goals are, we want them to identify those third-party groups that teach the skills and tools they need to be a top performer in our company and align with their personal goals.

DAN LEVITAN, MAVERON
Understanding What "Right" Looks Like

We look for people who have high character and integrity and are obsessed with new business models and finding innovation. We look for people who want to be partners and help great companies drive great financial results, not individuals who only want to be leaders of a venture firm or the companies we invest in. The entrepreneurs whose companies we back want to run their own show, and our partners have to be willing to let them.

Venture is a hard thing to predict. It's hard to say what the characteristics are that make great investors. The characteristics of a strong partner are:

- Having a solid point of view, while being a good listener.

- Being more interested in the right answer, than in being right.

- Being data driven and pragmatic.

- Being competitive yet supportive of their partners, and collaborative in getting to the right answer.

- Being aware of his or her strengths and weaknesses, and able to leverage those strengths while appropriately neutralizing weaknesses by seeking the strengths of others.

#CEOpov

We take a 'gang tackling' approach to many investments. It doesn't matter who finds it or who invests in it; what matters is that we create a replicable pipeline of great entrepreneurs and great investments. The VC world is very competitive. There are too many practitioners with too many dollars chasing too small a group of great entrepreneurs. As a result, most firms in the industry are average at best. It doesn't make sense to be in the industry unless you're in the top quartile or top decile. How do you get there? By finding what each person does at top-decile level and having them do it on a replicable basis.

As a small organization with only 15 employees, a good chunk of people are high potential. My job is to determine how best to individually nurture their potential. There are five things a VC must do to create a top-performing organization, and our best partners are self-aware of their strengths measured against the five:

1. Predicting the future

2. Finding companies and individuals who can take advantage of the trends that you see

3. Negotiating an appropriate investment with entrepreneurs

4. Mentoring and helping do whatever you can to accelerate the progress of those entrepreneurs

5. Being objective and thoughtful in when and how to monetize the investments

With high-potentials, my job is to grow their strengths as investors against those five measures. For example, maybe someone has a really good nose for finding good people. After they make two or three introductions to investments, and after the meetings I come away continuously impressed by those introductions, I may think, hmmm, this person is young, but they have a nose for good people. That's something for me to nurture.

Another example could be a person who makes highly insightful comments that shift the paradigm for how I, and the rest of our team, think through an investment. For that person, I would develop them further by reinforcing their input. I might note it for the semi-annual review so I can provide specific feedback of how they changed the mindset. I might come into the team meeting and acknowledge that their input created a good discussion of the team. I'd encourage the rest of the team to model that behavior.

Another way is, in these team settings, to ask people, 'What do you think?' They may be young and not an obvious partner, but my question shows that their contribution is valued.

There's always a risk of perceived favoritism, but who cares? Everyone in the organization needs to know that the leader is objective and there's a clear set of criteria. Favoritism has a negative connotation if people are playing politics and don't deserve the attention. But if everyone in our organization understands that our business is about finding great investments, and someone is replicable in finding them, my job as the leader is to favor them.

By definition, you are your track record, and your scorecard speaks for yourself. I learned to have my CFO deliver the scorecard, because he's impartial. The numbers speak for themselves. And this goes for leaders too. Great leaders acknowledge when they don't have great years or show weak performance. The leader's job is to observe and drive direction and set results, but to be viewed as objective. That means looking at one's self objectively and holding to the same standards to which we hold others. When I've let my team down, I've acknowledged it.

To develop our high-potential people, we make sure people on our investment team understand what 'right' looks like in terms of investments. We try to give them an inside track to see how things that are really working work. We want them to be able to have benchmarks to use.

A lot of our business is done at the board level. One thing we try to do is take our more junior people to the boardrooms of some of our best companies and show them how they work, and how the more successful creators of influence manage those board dynamics.

SUNNY GUPTA, APPTIO
Having a Deep Desire to Win

I look for people who are complete self-starters. We subscribe to a lot of the same values that Seahawks coach Pete Carroll used as the foundation for building a championship team. We like people who have chips on their shoulders. We have people who went to great-named schools, but frankly it's not about that. It's about being willing to go the extra mile for customers – to stay up those two extra hours to incorporate the next feature into the product, or pick up the phone and call that new prospect and persuade them that we are the best solution for their problems. We want people who have something to prove, and who have a deep, internal desire to win. That's a very hard thing to teach, so we recruit and develop leaders around that. The second part is experience. For certain critical roles, we may need to hire from outside, but generally, we want to develop leaders from within. We want to make sure we give them different experiences within the company to grow their skills.

I spend a lot of time doing doughnut and coffee sessions or skip one-on-ones with our high-potentials. I think it's a two-way experience. It's an opportunity for me to learn what's happening in the company and in their function, and it's important to continue to develop them in our leadership philosophy. I had lunch with one of our top performers who's been promoted every year and a half, but within the same function. I'm encouraging him to leave his job, even for a lateral move to another department, to gain new and different experience. You have to be well-rounded with complete experience in multiple functions in order to further your development and ultimately reach your potential. I do about two to four meetings like this a week.

There's a risk of perceived favoritism, but I look at it as we are growing quickly and the only way the company is going to scale is by having the leadership we need. It's my responsibility to employees and shareholders to identify the top talent of the company and develop them into the next tier of leaders. Favoritism doesn't cross my mind, because it's all about what's best for the company. I think people see me as someone who is fair and objective, and who lets the best argument win. In 20 years, when the story gets written about Apptio, I hope five or 10 or 15 CEOs have come out of this company.

Carmen Cook is our VP of people and culture. She worked with Larry Ellison at Oracle, then left and started doing organizational and leadership development. I met her about four years ago. I thought she'd be a great coach for me to work with, so I hired her for myself and realized what a great impact she was having. She had her own business and was coaching some of the top CEOs. It turned out we shared a mutual fascination for what coaching could do in a company like ours. Apptio was small – about 100 people. She really liked our culture and business model, and decided she wanted to go all in. Initially, I wasn't sure what she would do, but we were about culture and people and leadership, so we created her job. She has been instrumental and an incredible partner.

One of Carmen's primary responsibilities is leadership development, and she designed a program called Advanced Development Potentials (ADP), aimed at our high potentials. The leadership team nominates up to two people per department to participate, and those program participants are paired with executives on the leadership team and meet on a monthly basis.

We also conduct monthly leadership forums for our top company leaders, where we share best practices, what's working, what's not working. And for managers, we have a program that helps them become great managers. They learn the basics: how to write a review, give constructive feedback, deal with poor performers. You've heard this a million times, and we say it, too: We hire slow, fire fast. If we hired someone who's not a fit, we want to ensure that the mistake is dealt with and learned from quickly.

Enable Others to Act

PHYLLIS CAMPBELL, JP MORGAN CHASE
Thinking Locally, Acting Globally

We want the common characteristics that everyone wants in their leaders: Hard workers, who believe in putting the customer first and who walk the talk. We want people who want sustained growth within the company, because that's what's best for the longevity of a team and for keeping the best people.

We also want life-long learners. There are so many opportunities to learn through our internal training sessions. I truly learn something new every day. We want people to see the potential we offer for growth and the unlimited opportunities that exist in a global company.

Our future leaders are those who think locally but spend time in our global markets. The best way to accelerate your career here is to be mobile and get the global experience. Leadership competencies aren't the same as they were 20 years ago. People who are collaborators – who are willing to expand their repertoire and take risks – become extremely valuable in developing others. They become good coaches who bring others along.

A second angle: We look for our "Big D," diversity. We want people who are comfortable cross-culturally and who are interested in being transferred around the company at a global level. We look for explicit characteristics to build a group of future leaders who are diverse by gender, ethnicity and geography. These are traits we ask our team leaders to consider when promoting people.

Our list of high-potential people is both spoken and unspoken. We have a formal high-potential list of employees across business lines who perform in the top 10%. These employees are clearly identified at the middle-management level and are selected to go through the JP Morgan Leaders training program.

I have people I mentor, which means I interact with potential future leaders frequently and bring them in for special projects. That could mean serving on a community board on the company's behalf. That's a great way for me to provide leadership opportunities and watch how they handle them.

We're beginning to develop more structure around this but, since we're a relatively new business here, we've not yet established the process. I tend to spend time with those people who have been hired in the last five years and less time with our retail teams. It's time we put a process in place that sends the single, consistent message that 'you're valued and important.' We have business resource groups within the organization in which people are asked to take leadership roles and we have some volunteer groups that offer the same great opportunities for leadership development.

There's not much risk of perceived favoritism. We're very performance and value oriented. We have an accountable culture based on merit, so the people who live the values are very visible.

We talk a lot with our high-potentials and all our leaders. Jamie Dimon, CEO of JP Morgan Chase and based in New York, encourages the value of 'speak up'. Executives at the top don't have all the answers, and we encourage everyone to voice their ideas. We want to hear when things are going well and if there are ways to make them even better. And if something is going wrong, we want people to make it our problem or our issue. We want an empowered culture that believes we are all leaders, especially those closest to the customer. And as leaders, you always need to be challenging the status quo and most importantly, be able to defend your ideas. As a board member of Nordstrom, I know they use an upside down pyramid to illustrate the value of the customers and employees at the top of the pyramid.

MAUD DAUDON,
SEATTLE METROPOLITAN CHAMBER OF COMMERCE
Unleashing the Talent Around You

To be a leader, you have to be effective at unleashing the talent around you. You need to be able to put yourself in other's shoes – and understand what's going on for that person. A good leader is strategic and helps the team build on ideas to make them even better. A leader is compassionate and helps people get unstuck or overcome barriers. Not only is he or she able to uncover an individual's abilities, but also helps them realize their full capabilities.

Having said this, there is no 'one size fits all' characteristics of leadership. Different forms of leadership are needed and valued within organizations. Let me describe two leaders within the Chamber today who have different characteristics but who are both very effective.

One is super smart, a quick study on content, a systems thinker and able to manage multiple issues simultaneously. This person's demeanor is the servant-leader type: non-egotistical, supremely competent and very respectful. This person is not afraid to challenge ideas, or conventional thinking with a calm demeanor and a wicked sense of humor. Another is also smart, incredibly organized and disciplined. This person takes on major projects, manages them completely and comes in under budget.

The challenge is finding ways to keep motivating these leaders to ensure they stay interested in being part of the organization. In both of these cases, the leaders have taken on significant additional responsibilities, which have both challenged them and kept them on an active learning curve.

If you listen within the organization, you learn who are identified as natural leaders. You can figure out who is most highly regarded and why. This, coupled with one's own judgment, creates pathways for how to best deploy talent within an organization.

I don't spend a lot of *extra* time interacting with potential future leaders, because extra time is really at a limit. But there are so many teaching moments in the day-to-day of what we do, the interaction comes naturally and frequently. I do try to push people out of their comfort zones. I often try and delegate leadership roles in the community, for example.

#CEOpov

Favoritism is something I try hard to guard against. The key is to appreciate each person's value-add to the organization. I value diversity, and allow myself to appreciate differences.

We don't have a formal development program for high-potential managers, but we do have an executive coach who is available to senior leaders in the organization on an as-needed basis. If I see someone with high-potential struggling, I have found coaching to be a valuable tool. Some of our leaders have been 'coached out' of the organization and it has helped them go further faster with their careers.

RAY HEACOX, NBC KING 5
Allowing Insecurity to Drive Results

The people I'm looking for have to want it. They have to have goals, and an approach to the work and have some love for the kind of work we do. That's what motivates people. And they have to be a little insecure, because insecurity drives us whether we like it or not. For my money, the best people are people who are desperately trying to overcome whatever those insecurities are. They work twice as hard and push twice as much. They're conscious and constantly thinking about how to work with their own strengths and weaknesses. There's something about that level of insecurity that if harnessed in the right place at the right time can drive amazing behavior and be a powerful fuel for winning. It takes tremendous self-awareness to be successful at dealing with what drives you and use that self-knowledge to keep learning and improving.

I have a mental list of high-potentials – but I would never name them out loud in the real world. I don't set aside formal time to meet with high-potential people (except for my direct team), but coaching is really my job – it's every leader's job. It's where I prefer to spend my time. I work in a business where I don't physically do the work, they do. So my job is to make sure I help them do their best. I don't pretend to be the expert or to know everything. My job is to make sure the experts do their best job.

I meet with people for 60 minutes, in one-on-one discussion sessions that are strictly for coaching on issues that are important for them and important to me. Because I might meet with people in sales, news, engineering, finance and technology in any given day, I can't focus on any one thing. I have to help them think about what will make them better at their job. My job is to be a generalist, a good listener and able to absorb information quickly. It's the most fun and the most frustrating.

I invest in a person who shows a willingness to be introspective and has the smarts. They have to be willing to peel back the onion to understand who they are, and their strengths and weaknesses. If you aren't willing to step back and look closely, it'll be hard to grow. The best of the best are doing that self-analysis all the time. They're constantly asking themselves questions: Was I too aggressive? Did I offend that person? Because your natural insecurity causes you to question, and that makes you self-aware.

The truth of how you deal with your best performers is in the everyday interactions and coaching opportunities. I meet weekly, one-on-one with my direct reports. That's where we talk about the tactics of the business. And I meet monthly one-on-one with some next-level down managers, who are people with high-potential in key positions, such as the assistant news director or the director of digital sales. They don't report to me, but it's important that I interact with them regularly.

I will have ongoing one-on-one sessions with anyone who wants to have them with me. They have to take the initiative. Usually, I don't have more than a couple of takers in any given year. People generally feel uncomfortable and are reluctant in random meetings with executives. That's driven by the culture of some departments. But I like to break that down. My direct reports know my style and know I'm not meeting with their team members to create a problem. I'm doing it so we can all get better and to help me. The more I understand what's going on in the organization, the smarter I'll be when it comes time to make tough decisions.

It would not be perceived as favoritism because it's natural for me to meet with so many people in so many different positions throughout the day. To be brutally honest, there are employee groups that don't get the same amount of attention. Undoubtedly, I spend more time with news department than I do with technology. I trust our technology team to be really good at what they do and keep us on the air. It's not my expertise, and I can't make their decisions. And it's not that I don't trust the news department. It's just that by volume, on a daily basis, there's always so much going on that's changeable and strategic.

At the corporate level, Gannett offers tremendous amounts of training and tuition reimbursement. There's companywide training in sales and leadership. What's unique about a distributed organization like ours, meaning there are stations located all over the country, is that development is very local to the market. In the past year and a half, we went through a process at the corporate level similar to the Session C process at GE. It's a leadership development process that rates our high-potential employees on their current potential for promotion:

- Are they immediately promotable?
- Are they promotable in the next 1-2 years?
- Are they now in the highest position that we think they'll be able to attain? And then we rate on the performance in the current position they have.

If I think a particular employee has the basic skills, the brains and the ability to go up three more levels – but they're young and not ready to be promoted today – I look at them as being promotable in the next two years. I track their performance against time and the skills they need to acquire. Going through analysis of key people on a regular basis is pretty healthy. A development plan for someone who is hugely promotable with a long runway ahead is different than someone who has reached the highest position. That person's development plan might be much more focused on getting better skilled at their position, so they can be the best of the best doing what they do.

Encourage the Heart
JON BRIDGE, BEN BRIDGE JEWELER
Taking a Page From the Boy and Girl Scouts of America

We want nice people as our next leaders. It's a funny thing to say, but we want nice people who are competent in their job and passionate about our product. We take a page out of the Boy and Girl Scout creed in regards to honesty and trustworthiness, and people need to be eager to achieve.

About 10 years ago, my wife, Bobbe, and I got to know the local manager at our coffee shop in Magnolia. She was young and bubbly and excited. She had a solid crew of people, was involved in the neighborhood and knew all the customers, who all seemed very happy. She wanted to buy the business, but when that fell through, we hired her. She was a sales person in our flagship store in downtown Seattle, and she quickly built her clientele. She went through our training courses, and eventually applied for a manager's position. We opened a store in El Paso, Texas and she decided she wanted to move. Because she's so independent and knows how to build community and clients, she's doing great!

#CEOpov

We want people like her – people who are nice and excited, who care and want to move up. We can teach the fundamentals about jewelry. But we can't change a person's personality, their level of enthusiasm, how they deal with people or whether they care. In this business, you have to like people – all people. We've had staff who've had missteps in that area and we've had to terminate their employment. We take it very seriously.

If you're nice and empathetic, that solves so many problems. You don't teach those qualities easily – but you can help people stop and think before they act. We try to work on a lot of those things.

One way is by showing how much our leadership authentically cares. I call everyone on his or her birthday and anniversary and close to the day they start. My uncle did this when he was co-CEO with my dad. I thought it was kind of hokey, but now I get it. It is a way for me to show I sincerely care. Now, I want to do it because that's how you get to know people better.

We do reviews, and part of that is by going into the store and talking to the leader's colleagues. It's like a 360-degree review. One of our main goals is to make sure there's an open door. Our family's Navy background has given us a lot of positive things, and one of those things is maintaining a real open door policy. There's a three-pronged tradition in the Navy called the Captain's Mast when you come before officers for minor misconduct; to receive a medal or positive recognition; or with individual concerns or requests. The third one is the one we've implemented here. In the Navy you have a chain of command, but you can always talk to your commanding officer. Here, any of our associates can call me directly with work or personal concerns.

In addition, every night, one of our executive officers calls every single store. We rotate the job. Originally, we'd call to find out how the day's business was, but now that's all online. We still do it because it's a valuable part of our culture. We touch base regularly to find out if there was an opportunity to pat someone on the back, or if there's a problem we need to address.

I spend time with existing managers and supervisors, and those people we've earmarked to become managers and supervisors. We have an internal ladder, and our mangers work closely with our regional vice presidents to decide who will be their assistant manager. We keep an eye on our top salespeople to see if they show interest in developing as leaders.

Having the name Bridge may create resentment. But we expect our family members to be as competent as everyone else, if not more so. For example, Ed's kids may be on a fast track to be in management; that happens. But they have to love the business and prove themselves in the jobs they have just like everyone else. In fact, they have to be better than anyone else (and they are); that's the only way people will respect them.

One of my first memories coming to work here was when I pulled into the parking lot, and I didn't even have a parking spot. I was a little ticked, but my uncle kept everything equal. It was that way then, and is still that way now.

We have an education department and conduct various trainings including leadership. We bring employees in who've been identified as potential managers and supervisors. During a three-day session, we expose them to the inner-workings of the business. They learn business, operations and leadership with a clear focus on our values for how we treat people. We trust they'll go back to their respective stores and work hard to become assistant managers – then eventually managers and beyond.

#CEOpov

In terms of general education, we encourage each employee to take courses from the Gemological Institute of America and get certification in gemology. We pay for half of the courses up front, and they pay for half. Having skin in the game shows their commitment, and if they complete the degree, we reward them by refunding them the amount they paid, meaning we end up paying 100%.

JOHN OPPENHEIMER, COLUMBIA HOSPITALITY
Uncovering Leaders at All Levels

We look for enthusiastic people who go beyond the call of duty and take action faster than others. Those are the people who stand out. Our future leaders are smart, confident and willing to take chances. They look for ways to make things even better and are willing to tell us the bad news when something goes wrong.

I'm a big believer that business is not just business. I spend time getting to know future potential leaders better. Good leaders get to know each other and care about each other and understand each other's families and lives. The most interesting part of our business is the people, so the better you know them the better everything works in our business.

There's minimal risk of perceived favoritism because we practice the Golden Rule. We treat everyone with respect. I just may spend a little more time getting to know our rising leaders, but I'm nice to everyone. Leadership is not very complicated – it's simply being genuine, nice and caring.

We do three things to develop leaders. We look for the diamonds in the rough, meaning we look for the people who have the fire and are on a trajectory toward advancement. They could be in any position in the company, so we make sure we're uncovering them at all levels. Once we identify them, we spend time with our young leaders in a variety of experiences at a variety of venues. Lastly, we offer them additional leadership development opportunities in the Columbia Academy, our training and development program, which trains team members to exceed expectations all the time.

In addition, we listen to them. Part of developing great leaders is taking the time to listen. Up-and-comers often have the freshest, exciting ideas. If a person has high-potential chances are they're on the front lines dealing with guests every day. So who better to make informed, reasoned suggestions on how we can deliver better experiences to our guests?

PAMELA HINCKLEY, TOM DOUGLAS RESTAURANTS
Matching Opportunity with Great People

We look for energy and passion. We want people who are passionate about food and beverage and creating the ultimate guest experience. One of my heroes, Danny Meyers (a New York City restaurateur and the CEO of Union Square Hospitality Group, which includes the Gramercy Tavern and Union Square Grill), wrote a wonderful book on hiring the right people in hospitality. He looks for someone who has that innate heart that connects with guests. Some people are just born with a quality that you see in how they listen and look you in the eye with a smile. We can't create that, but we can support it with infrastructure and technology.

I have the Watch List of high-potential people. Those who get the endorsements aren't big surprises. They sparkle. You can see it when you do a quick walk-through a restaurant. They seek you out. The company is still small enough that employees can and should build a relationship with Tom. I think he misses that direct contact with people. I encourage people to call him, ask him to coffee, though he prefers a glass of scotch.

#CEOpov

There's a risk of perceived favoritism, but as we've grown, we've become more measured in our hiring process to make sure to look at a broad array of candidates, even though we have a short list in our heads. And by being that thorough, there have been some very pleasant surprises.

To develop our high-potential managers, we have the Sprout Program. Every other month, our core leadership visits each property to discuss the challenges, successes and identify up-and-coming leaders who could become potential candidates for promotions or other positions. We want to spread the talent around by matching the business opportunities we have with our great people.

For example, Assembly Hall in South Lake Union, is our most complex project to date. It has a specialty grocery store, a Japanese American café and a juice and coffee bar. We had to hire nearly 100 people, as well as draw from existing managers and our Sprout list to move people and promote people into positions that help us cultivate our culture. That opened up a lot of opportunities for others to move around and be promoted. It's like a gigantic chess board where we try to find the best fit for our best people. We don't always get it right the first time, but we keep trying until we do.

DAN PRICE, GRAVITY PAYMENTS
Committing To Find a Way

I look for passion – but not just passion in general. I look for people who are passionate about moving forward and getting to the next thing. I look for someone who really thinks outside the box – and challenges themselves, not on *can* I do this, but *how* am I going to do this. I look for the commitment to find a way.

I also look for people who really see themselves as a steward, who take a high level of responsibility for our stakeholders and customers. Our customers are number one and I look for people who understand the huge degree of responsibility we have in serving them. We manage $5 billion dollars for small and independent businesses. Without us taking that responsibility, the whole independent business region could shut down. We're the rails – and we need to take that really seriously. People in companies that have come before us took advantage of that role. They saw it as power and imposed a few more taxes here and there than what was in the original agreement. Our approach is to see this as an opportunity to serve our customers, not to be an owner or an overlord.

I have a mental list of potential leaders – and it gets updated daily. I've learned to expect to be very surprised. I try to be really open-minded and collect a lot of information. I look at people over the long run. People are people, and we are infinitely creative and able to change. Not that we *will* change, but it's a possibility, so I think staying open minded is important.

If, as a team, we don't see someone as a potential leader they're probably not a good fit for the company. Because we are growing so fast, I think that becomes mutually clear fairly quickly. We really need almost everyone on that high-potential track.

Now, in my mind leadership doesn't mean a certain spot on the org chart or management or supervisory type capabilities. One of the best leaders we've ever had in the company is a frontline tech support person. He doesn't like management. He'd be good at it, but he's not interested. But there are other people who want it and will be even better.

If someone is here, I owe him or her a certain amount of time, attention and energy. We do as a team. We have an Employee Bill of Rights that lays out what employees should expect from the standpoint of leadership development and transparency. I interact very regularly with everyone (all 105 employees) here in the company.

To some degree, all the big decisions are made in consultation with the entire team (company). In order to maintain this as we grow, we know we have to be very, very transparent and build business procedures, processes and infrastructure around transparency. And then we have to over-communicate what the strategy is and what we're looking for from everyone, because this approach is so different then other companies.

Leaders might have their door open, but you can't just have your door open. You have to be constantly saying, 'Hey, I'd be really excited if you walked though this door.' Excitement might come across in different ways. It might mean I debate you toe-to-toe, and that might be uncomfortable for you, but that's me respecting you as a person. No one wants me to nod my head and blow you off and not really take the time to hear what you have to say or take it into consideration.

For the first seven or eight years, I was very careful not to have any personal relationships at work. Probably two or three years ago I decided that I was going to start building more personal relationships. It was partly for selfish reasons, because I enjoy getting to know the people who I work with.

My original thought on that came from thinking that people deserved to have a boss, and I couldn't be both a boss and a friend. I'm not necessarily saying I *can* be both of those things, but the line just became a lower priority. I still have a high degree of respect for people's privacy and their personal time, but taking someone to lunch and just talking about what's going on in their life or in my life is something I'm open to doing now, where I wasn't before.

I think I assumed having those types of relationships would be negative from a business standpoint, but I haven't experienced any significant business consequences. In fact, it's been really positive. Some of the people here viewed me in an iconic or heroic sense – as opposed to just a person – and those expectations were sometimes hard to live up to. This approach has helped me erode those expectations. We have smart, ambitious people here, so instead of looking to me or expecting me to fill in the gaps, they are empowered to fill those gaps.

To develop high-potential managers, we have the MAP program, which is a 12-13 month course, with a curriculum that we developed in house. It has different modules, such as understanding yourself, negotiating, having difficult conversations at work, judgment and decision-making – those type of topics. We cover about one topic a month through a seminar and reading and small groups or peer-to-peer mentorships. The program is optional for everyone, but it's strongly encouraged for those who have management responsibility.

We believe 70-80% of leadership and personal development come from experience learning on the job – and not from these academic programs. We also have about 15-20 people in a coaching program. They can work with an executive coach who meets with people on a confidential basis. We believe the practical learning – the learning by doing – is most important.

DEVELOPING LEADERS, A JOB THAT'S NEVER DONE

There is nothing about developing the next generation that today's leaders take for granted. Instead, the search for high-potential talent, and the commitment to developing that talent, is a constant high priority.

#CEOpov

All the leaders I spoke with have a mental list (and sometimes a literal list) of the high-potential people working for them. And through a series of lunches, meetings, assignments, opportunities, training and questions they are working to develop each one.

But that's about where the similarities end. While one leader seeks people with keen interpersonal skills, another seeks people with an innate desire to win, and still another wants people willing to take risks and challenge the status quo. And all those approaches are 'right' because each reflects the specific values — and therefore the culture — of the organization. In other words, leadership development — like leadership itself — is a highly individual thing. And, like leadership itself, it's vital to any organization's success. Take a second to think about your own style of developing the leaders around you.

IN YOUR OWN WORDS

1.   Do you have a list of high-potential people in your head?

_____

_____

_____

2.   What qualities do you look for? How do you assess for those qualities?

_____

_____

_____

3.   What experiences, mistakes and failures were most helpful to you in developing your own leadership skills? How do you impart that wisdom?

_____

_____

_____

4.   What are you doing, formally and informally, to help develop the high-potential people in your organization?

_____

_____

_____

5.   Is your leadership development process consistent with the organization's values? If so, how? If not, what do you need to do to make it so?

_____

_____

_____

PART 5: FROM THEIR PERSPECTIVE: INSIGHTS FOR EMERGING LEADERS

Change. Everything – everything – is changing at rates faster than ever before, and we all have to deal with it. Sometimes the changes are pretty minor irritations (it's not your imagination – that box of your favorite cereal *is* smaller) and other times much more serious. (Climate change…anyone?).

Small or large, today's leaders have to do much more than just deal with the changes happening at breakneck speed. Leaders must anticipate change, plan for change, manage change and – the hardest part of all – actually CHANGE while not missing a beat. And doing so gets more challenging every day.

Technology is the most prominent driver of change. Having the skills to understand technology, the opportunities it creates and the pace with which it changes – coupled with navigating the staggering amount of information generated, manipulated and stored – are amongst the greatest challenges facing today's leaders and those to follow them.

But technology – huge as it is – isn't the only driver of massive change. Other contributors include globalization, emerging economies, changing demographics and, yep, the weather. All of that requires a new set of competencies in addition to those that are *already* required.

You could forgive top leaders if, in the face of all that, they were at a loss for words. But in fact, they were not. Instead, they had a lot of words to share – valuable insight and advice about the key challenges facing leaders, essential qualities for leadership and the derailers most likely to result in leadership failure.

THE MOST DAUNTING CHALLENGES

Given how much change we face, it isn't surprising that when asked to identify the greatest challenge facing future leaders almost every person I spoke to chose something different.

Adapting New Leadership
Ted Baseler, Ste. Michelle Wine Estates:

Fifty years ago, leadership was dictatorial or more military-style. Times have changed. Today, a good leader guides not directs, and inspires not commands. Understanding that shift, and what it means to their responsibility as leaders and to supporting a team is vital.

Different styles can be effective in different circumstances. Very charismatic leaders can rally people into an assembly of excitement and screaming and yelling and foot stomping. There are quiet leaders who lead by example and are just as effective. The key ingredient to leadership is giving the credit to other people.

Josh Dirks, Project Bionic:

Mahogany Row is over. Leadership is no longer defined by tenure. Today, we see more 20-somethings running bigger companies, and so the very idea of leadership has changed.

Engaging and Motivating People
Jon Bridge, Ben Bridge Jeweler:

We live in a fast-paced world, in which people are not necessarily loyal to the company. Leaders have to find ways to engage and motivate people who have the attention span of a fly.

Finding Balance
Maud Daudon, Seattle Metropolitan Chamber of Commerce:

Leaders are challenged to make the fast-paced work environment fair for everyone and to create success for employees while at the same time creating success for the organization.

Dr. Paul Ramsey, UW Medicine:

In healthcare, the biggest challenge leaders face is that everything we do is changing faster than it ever has in human history – from research to healthcare delivery to reimbursement policies and practices. There is a need to change our educational programs to keep pace with the changes in our knowledge base and our clinical practice imperatives. Technology is enabling biomedical research to change far faster than it ever has. This means that we're discovering knowledge faster, and we need to translate the knowledge to better care and better health while also focusing on cost control.

The rapid pace of change means that we also need to pay more attention to the wellness and 'balance' of our employees. Too many individuals are working harder and harder. We are actively supporting multiple approaches to improve individual employee wellness and mentorship programs that include support for balance between one's professional and personal activities. When I'm counseling individuals, especially those who report directly to me, I make a major effort to help them find an approach to achieve balance in their lives. Leaders burn out when they can't achieve balance. And employees look to their leaders to set an example in finding balance. It's important that employees see balance as a priority.

Mastering Integrative Thinking

Norm Rice, Seattle Foundation:

We need to break down silos. Leaders need to foster integrative thinking and leverage people's broader skills. We need multi-talented people to run an organization and to be engaged in the broader view.

The Internal Battle

Dan Price, Gravity Payments:

The internal battle is the hardest and most interesting one. It's hard to define and is unique to everyone, but it's the self-discipline, making choices, being rational – getting outside of yourself and making decisions on what you want your life to be or how you want to approach your life. And then problem-solving and troubleshooting, the things that get in your way, be it anxiety, depression, exuberance, greed, fear, complacency – there are so many things that can be disruptive to leaders. I argue you are your own biggest asset and you're your own biggest enemy. How you perform internally has a huge impact on how you perform externally.

Pamela Hinckley, Tom Douglas Restaurants:

Once they've identified that this is the correct industry for them, we want people to want to give it their all. There are a lot of glittery opportunities out there in other industries (like technology and finance), but if hospitality is your calling, you have to say YES! However, this business is not easy. It requires working days and nights and weekends, and you have to be sure that your values fit the required professional, time and lifestyle commitment. This industry is not for everyone. I've had some fierce conversations with people who are attracted to this company but want the 9-5 schedule. That is not going to put you on a leadership track.

Simplifying Complexity

Father Stephen Sundborg, Seattle University

The biggest challenge facing leaders of complex organizations like ours is how to unify it, give it vision and inspire people with that vision. This university is far more complex than when I started 17 years ago, as a result of technology, regulation, and the changing landscape of students. Student expectations and demands bring about huge complexity. They expect universities to respond to every dimension of their development, their growth, and their needs. Technology has multiplied that complexity, rather than simplified it. Anything you deal with gets out to so many people so quickly, which means the issues you're dealing with involve many more people than in the past.

Keeping Committed

Dan Levitan, Maveron:

People pour their heart and soul into something, and unless things happen quickly, some people get frustrated and abandon it. Instead, of recognizing the opportunity, they go off and look for the next thing because this month or year hasn't gone well. I see people in some of our portfolio companies do this. They're at a great company; they have great managers and a phenomenal leader. But they get impatient. They don't understand the opportunity that's in front of them. There's so much they could learn, and they could be associated with the success of a company going from obscurity to ubiquity – like Apple or Starbucks.

Creating a Great Culture
John Oppenheimer, Columbia Hospitality:

Leaders must create a five-star culture that attracts the right people, and makes their company people's first choice for employment. It's hard to create a great place to work when the bar for great workplaces gets higher every day. Leaders need to be evangelical about their passion for what they do. In turn, they create a work environment where team members become evangelists about their experiences working here. We want them to love working in this organization. We won't settle for 'satisfied.' That's a C in a grade book. If a leader in our business is pleased with satisfied that's a *fail*. We need to constantly strive to create experiences – starting with team members – who inspire people to want to be our evangelists. That's what translates into their longevity with the company, the happiest guests and the most fun for everyone every day.

Embracing the Three Ts: Technology, Time and Thinking
Scott Oki, Oki Developments:

We must be willing and smart enough to embrace technology and figure out how it can best be used and deployed. The pace of change is the biggest challenge; things are happening at warp speed.

John Rubino, GreenRubino:

The biggest challenge is time, as a multi-dimensional idea. We are in a 'right now' environment because of technology. Email, social media, all those things create pressure to deliver, decide and act without taking time to think. There's a lack of patience from clients, from senior executives, from board members, from investors. The opportunity to take time to reflect and learn from mistakes doesn't exist. We just move on to the next project.

Ray Heacox, NBC KING 5:

I honestly believe time has gotten shorter. Not as in, I'm older so time gets shorter, but the fact is that time in our business is shorter. You get less time to focus. To be competitive, you have to move fast and make millions of decisions and you're not going to make them all correctly. You're going to make mistakes, but that doesn't slow time down. It's become clear to me that you can't do it all. You have to pick a few things to focus on, and that's hard. You can't not do Facebook or not do Twitter. You have to do all those things, but the place you might need to spend the overwhelming time is focused on the bigger picture of how to make your whole organization really good.

Balancing Priorities
Brad Tilden, Alaska Airlines

The challenge for today's leaders and those who are up and coming is they're drinking from a fire hose. At Alaska, a leader has many tactical things they have to do, like launching flights, training pilots or flight attendants, fixing airplanes, or closing the books. Airlines are dynamic, so there's always something happening that's changing our world. Leaders have to get the job done, and manage all the new things coming at them from outside. And then strategically, the company has to drive change itself, so we can continue to differentiate ourselves and bring fares down to attract new customers. It's a real challenge for leaders to stay on top of the day-to-day stuff, think strategically, and maintain some semblance of balance! We need to be good at prioritizing, good at getting things done quickly, and sometimes good at saying no.

Being Decisive

Greg Rankich, Xtreme Consulting:

There's so much information out there, and people get over-whelmed. It's like they're stuck in molasses when it comes to making decisions. I recently joined the board of a startup with a 30-something CEO. The younger generation has the advantage of growing up with technology, which can be a big advantage, but you still have to make decisions. At one point, I had to tell him to stop overanalyzing and listening to other people. He needed to go with his gut and make a decision. To me, 5% profit is better than 0%. Be the scrappy underdog and scratch and claw to get revenue in the door, because when you get revenue in the door, that can lead to 10 other things that are going to be much more profitable. You don't get there by over-researching, overanalyzing and trying to be perfect.

Finding the Right Mentor

Sunny Gupta, Apptio

Up-and-comers don't get enough constructive feedback and coach-ing. Leadership is an evolution. You don't wake up one day and decide to be a leader; it's something that you learn and earn. As you're starting down your leadership path, you have to have people around you who are willing to take the time, invest in you and be open and honest in their criticism. One of the best learning opportunities is when mistakes get made, but if you never get that direct feedback in the moment, you can't improve or course-correct. Having a great coach or mentor who will be transparent with you and give you that feedback is critical and it's the area I see most young leaders struggle with, because generally people are not transparent, open and honest.

Making Mistakes and Learning
Phyllis Campbell, JP Morgan Chase

As a leader, by definition, you're out there taking more visible swings. The best baseball players hit .375 – .400, which is a great average. However, that also means they aren't always perfect. The best leaders admit mistakes and learn. They internalize the lesson, but not the guilt. They must be resilient, because we all make mistakes. The best leaders have the optimism and vision to keep their eye on the long ball – to know where they and their organizations are headed.

THE ONE 'MUST HAVE'

In addition, I asked each leader to name one leadership behavior or trait (besides integrity), that is a 'must have' for every leader. The biggest challenge for almost everyone was naming just one, and very few leaders named the same one.

Here are a handful of "must haves" in their own words:

Confidence
Ted Baseler, Ste. Michelle Wine Estates:

Being wishy-washy does not equal leadership. I find it amazing how some people will go through the pros and cons of a decision over and over. A military leader once said, 'Leadership is being confident even when you're not.' This doesn't mean overconfident, but it does mean being decisive. Once you have the research and the data, a good leader makes a decision. We don't know if it's right, but once the decision is made, be confident and implement it.

Empathy

Jon Bridge, Ben Bridge Jeweler:

The most important word in the human language is empathy. Leaders are out in front leading; they don't stand behind. And people work *with* them, not *for* them. They think before they ask someone to do something, and place themselves in the shoes of others. It works that way in personal relationships, too – like marriage. Empathy allows you to bite your tongue before you open your mouth. It means you think about how the person will feel when they hear the words you say. Taking time to really care is the best way to get the best out of people.

Active Listening

Phyllis Campbell, JP Morgan Chase:

Leaders are always about working with people and listening to bring the best ideas forward and the best people along. It comes from the servant-leadership model. We don't have all the answers; so listen.

Self-Awareness

Josh Dirks, Project Bionic:

Business leaders must be very self-aware and recognize the importance of being hard on themselves. To be a great leader, you have to have the ability to self-reflect. You have to be able to grade yourself on your own performance. I see a lot of leaders who persuade themselves they're not the problem, or that they're creating the solution. Very often, that's not the case. So unless you can be real and transparent with yourself in how you measure your own performance and your own strengths and weaknesses, then you can't help other people grow and develop into leaders.

Humor
Maud Daudon, Seattle Metropolitan Chamber of Commerce:

It's important to have a sense of humor and maintain levity through whatever adversity you're facing. Otherwise, work can be deadly. Humor is also a very humanizing thing. People who are really good with humor use it very effectively to disarm and unify. It's joyful – and can bring people to a different place.

Risk Assessment
Scott Oki, Oki Developments:

Besides passion, every leader should have the ability to assess risk; really understanding the potential downside is critical. I think it's something you can't learn from a textbook. You have to have a sense of what the ingredients are that impact a decision and be able to answer whether they are aligned in a way that allows for a good or bad outcome.

Persistence
Dan Levitan, Maveron:

I think extraordinary things can be accomplished over time – if people have resiliency and tenacity. Favoring process, rather than near-term outcomes, I think leaders have to take a longer view. One of my favorite quotes is by Danny Shader, founder and CEO of PayNearMe, one of the companies we had the privilege to back. He said: "Start ups fail for only one of two reasons. They run out of money or they run out of heart." I think great leaders should never run out of heart and persistence.

Passion
Brad Tilden, Alaska Airlines:

I love passion: Passion about the company, the industry, or whatever it is that you do – I just think you can do so much with it. It makes people fun to be around, and it's important for everyone to enjoy their work. I also see that 'self-correcting' notion in passionate people. They'll try something, and if it doesn't work, they'll try the next thing.

Vision
Greg Rankich, Xtreme Consulting:

Vision. It's easy to get caught in the day-to-day minutia. It's critical to keep looking at the bigger picture, to keep your eye on where you're headed and to make decisions that get you there.

Love
Dan Price, Gravity Payments:

Some people would be more comfortable with the word *passion*, but I actually think the word *love* is better. In its worst form and best form, it's always the exact opposite of apathy, and no leader should possess apathy. Because the challenges are so diverse and ever-changing, I think love is the one characteristic that can overcome all those challenges. Other characteristics may be more effective or appropriate for one challenge, but not well suited for the next item on the list. Love is the umbrella. To add more color, some people would say commitment or passion – but my lexicon's a little different than theirs.

They asked Che Guevara, arguably one of the most brutal terrorists that existed on earth, 'What's the number one characteristic you look for in a guerrilla fighter terrorist?' He answered: "At the risk of seeming ridiculous, let me say that the true revolutionary is guided by a great feeling of love. It is impossible to think of a genuine revolutionary lacking this quality."

I really believe love is the number one thing that can help you in anything you do. It's *that* powerful. And it can be channeled for evil, because it's the one thing that blurs out everything. So self-skepticism is an important counter.

Humility
Ray Heacox, NBC King 5:

Great leaders can pull themselves out of the equation. They can look at the world in a way that allows them to see what other people can do. Lots of good leaders are egocentric. It's about power sometimes, influence sometimes – there are lots of components to good leadership that use that strong ego. The greatest leaders are almost always the ones who can back away from their ego and focus on what the people they're leading are capable of and empowering them to do it better.

Transparency
Sunny Gupta, Apptio:

Without transparency, you can't survive in this company and more companies are developing that kind of culture. You have to be open and honest. You can't talk behind people's backs; you have to talk to each other. You have to be transparent with employees, or customers, or the board. If you're not transparent and hold information back, you can't survive here and have no chance of becoming a leader.

Authenticity
Father Stephen Sundborg, Seattle University:

Authenticity means there's coherence between how you act and who you are, which is vital. Authenticity or transparency means what you see is what you get. There's no hidden agenda.

Pamela Hinckley, Tom Douglas Restaurants:

Authentic engagement. You have to have the ability to listen honestly and respond authentically, without political motivation or harboring a secret agenda.

DERAILERS CAUSE FAILURE

I also asked each person to identify the behaviors or traits they commonly see derailing leaders. Collectively, arrogance – or some form of it – topped the list:

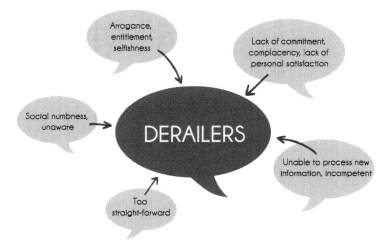

But leaders see all kinds of derailing behaviors and traits. Here are some in their own words:

No One Likes a Know-it-All

Ted Baseler, Ste. Michelle Wine Estates:

You can't be so confident that you think you're bullet proof; the leaders of businesses, non-profits, sports teams, and universities who get into trouble lack humility. Arrogance happens when people think the past will create future success. When they think they are the only ones who have the right answer, that they're smarter. It's the, 'I'm right you're wrong' mentality. That's when companies get into trouble.

Greg Rankich, Xtreme Consulting:

Title doesn't make you a leader, and being a know-it-all doesn't win friends. When you're a new leader in an organization, you have to trust your team and let them teach you. Believing you know it all hurts the team, hurts your potential – and is a path to failure.

Ray Heacox, NBC King 5:

Ego. Impatience for people who 'don't' think like I do' or aren't 'as smart as I am.'

Sunny Gupta, Apptio:

Being a 'know it all.'

Pamela Hinckley, Tom Douglas Restaurants:

Not willing to explore and think in terms of 'What if?' We are always challenged by Tom to do better. He's not one who's easily (ever) satisfied. For some, they take it personally, or they're rigid and uncomfortable in an environment where the quest for excellence is constant. You have to be willing to take risks and understand there are many ways to think about things.

I like to hire people who are different from me. When we work on a new concept, I like to test it on a wide range of audiences to make sure it's a sound idea worth pursuing. We poached someone on our finance team from another restaurant group, which was very bottom-line driven and disciplined. About halfway into his first year here, he gained the confidence to tell me that we run the company differently than what he was used to and different from the way he would do things. I appreciate that. I see it as we're both benefitting from mutual learning. He's teaching us about finance, and I value the skills, expertise and perspective he brings. And we're opening his eyes to our approach to business, which isn't always based on finances first.

Phyllis Campbell, JP Morgan Chase:

People get complacent, get arrogant and become ineffective. No one has the market on the best ideas, so it's required to work together and collaborate to find them. It takes patience and the ability to encourage people to provide feedback. Someone whose ego is in the way thinks they have all the answers; that they've 'arrived'. You have to check against this all the time. We make mistakes. We don't have all the answers. Be humble.

Taking Credit: In Other Words, Still Arrogance

John Oppenheimer, Columbia Hospitality:

When the *I*s in a sentence are too close together – "I did this or I did that" – derailment starts to happen real fast. People's egos get in the way of their success. This happens time and time again. Leaders need to remember it's all about *you*, not *me*. When leaders celebrate their own success, instead of the team's success, failure is looming. As leaders we must always ask whether we're leading because of our position or because we're genuine leaders. There's a big difference being in a position of leadership versus having earned the right to lead and thus be respected.

Norm Rice, Seattle Foundation:

One of the biggest problems for some leaders is the inability to let go. I think that comes from insecurity, from someone who feels if he or she is not involved or engaged in everything, he or she is not leading. So you become more focused on the execution than the delivery of the results. You know the old saying by President

Truman: 'It is amazing what you can accomplish if you don't care who gets the credit.' Great leaders think that way.

Dan Levitan, Maveron:

I see many people challenged by being an individual contributor and taking credit, versus being part of a team. A good leader is decisive and leads by example. He or she lets others take credit or give credit versus acting like he or she needs or wants it.

I've seen lots of cases where the up and coming leaders aren't able to balance their qualitative contribution with their quantitative contribution. They act like the contribution to the business is bigger than the numbers show, and they want to ignore some of the data. Sometimes it's tied to arrogance; sometime there's a gap between how they perceive themselves and how others perceive them.

And still a few others…

Social Numbness

John Rubino, GreenRubino:

Social numbness caused by technology. Recently, I was in New York (though it happens everywhere) and all I saw were people walking around the streets, on their phones texting, face down, unaware of their surroundings, crossing streets, almost getting hit by cabs. This myopic focus is dangerous. The more technology becomes ingrained at a younger age, the more people rely on social media and apps to communicate. We're creating inward communication instead of outward, and I think it could be a real problem that derails the successful development of future leaders.

Lacking Commitment

Scott Oki, Oki Developments:

Whether it's someone I want on a board or want to hire, I want to know they're in it for the long haul.

Lacking Vision

Brad Tilden, Alaska Airlines:

Leaders who spend time fighting the fires of the day, instead of stepping back and leading, will get derailed quickly. You can't get so caught in the weeds that you don't see the view from 30,000 feet.

It Takes a Lot To Be a Leader

Clearly, being a leader isn't easy. Leaders face innumerable challenges, and the number and pace of those challenges is growing exponentially. There are many qualities that leaders must have (almost as many qualities as there are leaders, it seems), and there are many ways in which leaders can derail and fail.

Still, it is possible to lead effectively. None of the people I spoke with would ever claim to be perfect, but by any measure they are successful. They make it work because they are constantly challenging themselves, learning and growing. And they have aligned their core values with the organizations they lead. Take a second to think about how you rate by these same measures.

IN YOUR OWN WORDS

1. On a scale of 1-10, how self-aware do you think you are as a leader? What do you think is your best leadership trait? Why?

    _____

    _____

    _____

2. What one quality do you think every leader must have? How do you assess for that quality when hiring or promoting others?

    _____

    _____

    _____

3. Did the must-have qualities named by the leaders impact your thinking in any way? If so, how?

    _____

    _____

    _____

4. Which qualities or behaviors have you seen most often derail leaders? Do you see that behavior in yourself? What do you think you need to stop doing to be a better leader?

    _____

    _____

    _____

5. How has technology challenged you as a leader? What do you need to do to manage the pace of change?

    _____

    _____

    _____

PART 6: MORE ON THE LEADERS

ALASKA AIRLINES, BRAD TILDEN

Alaska Air Group (NYSE: ALK) includes Alaska Airlines and Horizon Air. Alaska Airlines is the nation's seventh-largest airline, with 10,200 employees, 65 destinations (throughout the US, Canada and Mexico) and 131 aircraft. Regional carrier Horizon Air has 2,800 employees and 51 aircraft, which serve 39 cities across California, Idaho, Montana, Nevada, Oregon, Washington, Canada and Mexico.

- 13,000 employees
- Annual revenue: $5.2 billion
- Percentage of revenue spent on leadership development: NA
- www.alaskaair.com

Brad Tilden, President and CEO

Brad is president and chief executive officer of Alaska Airlines and Alaska Air Group, and CEO of Horizon Air.

Brad previously served as Alaska Air Group's chief financial officer and executive vice president of finance, leading the finance, information technology, planning, revenue management and corporate real estate organizations. Before joining Alaska in 1991, he spent eight years with the accounting firm Price Waterhouse at its offices in Seattle and Melbourne, Australia.

Brad earned a bachelor's degree in business administration from Pacific Lutheran University and an executive master's degree in business administration from the University of Washington. He also holds a private pilot's license. Brad is a director of Flow International Corp. and serves on the boards of Pacific Lutheran University and the Chief Seattle Council of the Boy Scouts of America, where he serves as council president.

A resident of Seattle, Brad is married and has three children.

APPTIO,
SUNNY GUPTA

Apptio is an independent provider of on-demand technology business management (TBM) solutions for managing the business of IT. Apptio enables IT leaders to manage the cost, quality and value of IT services by providing visibility into the total cost of IT services, communicating the value of IT to the business through an interactive Bill of IT™, and strategically aligning the planning, budgeting and forecasting processes. Global enterprise customers include Bank of America, Boeing, JPMorgan Chase, Microsoft, and Swiss Re.

- 450 employees
- Annual revenue: NA
- Percentage of revenue spent on leadership development: NA
- www.apptio.com

Sunny Gupta, CEO

Sunny is the co-founder, president and CEO of Apptio, responsible for company vision, strategic direction, planning and execution. Sunny's enterprise software career spans more than 20 years, with roles in general management, strategic marketing, product management and business development. Before founding Apptio, Sunny was executive vice president of products at Opsware and was responsible for all of Opsware product businesses up to its acquisition by Hewlett-Packard for more than $1.6 billion.

Sunny co-founded iConclude and created the IT runbook automation market. Sunny served as the company's CEO, serving such customers as ACS, Alaska Airlines, GlaxoSmithKline and Halliburton, until its acquisition by Opsware. Previously, Sunny held senior leadership roles in products, business development and engineering at Mercury Interactive, Rational Software, and IBM. Sunny earned a BS in computer science from the University of South Carolina. He was named Ernst & Young Entrepreneur of The Year in 2012.

#CEOpov

BEN BRIDGE JEWELER, JON BRIDGE

Ben Bridge Jeweler has more than 75 stores in 11 states and the province of British Columbia.

- 850 employees
- Annual Revenue: NA
- Percentage of revenue spent on leadership development: NA
- www.benbridge.com

Jon Bridge, Co-CEO & General Counsel

Since 1991, Jon has served as Co-CEO/General Counsel for Ben Bridge Jeweler, Inc., one of the largest family-run businesses in the state of Washington. Jon's great-grandfather, watchmaker Sam Silverman, opened the store's doors in 1912. During the 1920s, he sold the store to son-in-law Ben Bridge and the Bridge's have run the business ever since.

Tradition runs deep in the Bridge family. Jon is third-generation Navy. He was Navy Judge Advocate General's Corps (JAGC), a captain with nine years active-duty service and 22 in the reserve. Today, Jon continues to teach military law to ROTC midshipmen. Jon is a member of the Washington State Bar Association (former chair of the Legal Assistance to Military Personnel - LAMP Section); ABA (chair of the Military Law Committee), and King County Bar Association. He is a board member of Jewelers Mutual Insurance Company and Jewelers of America Political Action Committee.

As a community leader, Jon chairs the Alliance for Education and is on the boards of the Metropolitan Seattle Chamber of Commerce, the Association of Washington Business, Washington Historical Courts, and Evergreen Children's Association. He is also a member of Seattle Rotary. A Seattle native, he's a graduate of Garfield High School. He graduated magna cum laude with an honors degree in economics from the University of Washington in 1972 and earned his juris doctor from the UW Law School in 1976. Jon is married to Bobbe Bridge, a retired Justice of the Washington State Supreme Court who is the founding president and CEO of the Center for Children and Youth Justice. They have two adult children, Don (married to Sarah) and Rebecca (married to Evan), and two grand-daughters, Chloé and Emma.

COLUMBIA HOSPITALITY, JOHN OPPENHEIMER

Columbia Hospitality, Inc., a Seattle-based hospitality management and consulting firm, was founded in1995 by John Oppenheimer. Columbia's growing portfolio includes the award-winning boutique hotels of the Columbia Collection, conference centers, golf courses and distinctive venues. The company's continued success has led to an international expansion of the consulting division and more than 100 hospitality projects worldwide.

- 1,200 employees
- Annual revenue: NA
- Percentage of revenue spent on leadership development: NA
- www.columbiahospitality.com

John Oppenheimer, CEO

John is a travel and tourism entrepreneur with a passion for the hospitality industry. Over the past 25 years he has founded five successful, private hospitality-related businesses. He founded Columbia Hospitality in 1995 to manage Bell Harbor International Conference Center for the Port of Seattle. Bringing the company to immediate success, John led the acquisition of a premier portfolio of full-service, independent, upscale boutique hotels, conference centers, golf courses and unique venues. He established the company's active consulting division, which has completed projects for hospitality developments throughout the US and in Canada, Mexico, Portugal and the United Kingdom.

John currently serves on the Virginia Mason Medical Center Foundation board, the Western Region Advisory Board of Northern Trust, and is a member of the World President's Organization. John and his wife, Deanna, are past honorees of Seattle Hotel

Association's Evening of Hope Gala and have served as co-chairs of many civic events, including the Woodland Park Zoo Jungle Party, Virginia Mason's Dare to Dream Gala, and the Junior Achievement Puget Sound Business Hall of Fame event.

John graduated from the University of Puget Sound with degrees in urban affairs and political science.

GRAVITY PAYMENTS, DAN PRICE

Gravity Payments processes credit card payments for more than 10,000 merchants across the United States.

- 105 employees
- Annual revenue: NA
- Percentage of revenue spent on leadership development: NA
- www.gravitypayments.com

Dan Price, CEO

Dan founded Gravity Payments in 2004 in his Seattle Pacific University dorm room, when he was only 19. With the help of his older brother, Dan set up the payment-processing business and began serving small Seattle-area restaurant and retail businesses. By the time he was 23, his business had expanded to serve customers nationwide. Nine years after its dorm-room founding, Gravity Payments is among the top 50 credit card processors in the U.S. with customers in all 50 states.

Dan's innovative approach and contributions to the small business community have earned him prestigious awards, such as the 2010 SBA Young Entrepreneur of the Year Award, 2013 GeekWire Young Entrepreneur of the Year Award, 2009 Seattle Mayor's Small Business Award, and *Puget Sound Business Journal's* 40 under 40. Dan has been chronicled in *Entrepreneur Magazine, Inc. Magazine, Yahoo! Finance, Wall Street Journal, Seattle Times, Puget Sound Business Journal, Seattle Business Monthly, Business Week, GeekWire* and *Forbes*.

GREENRUBINO, JOHN RUBINO

GreenRubino is a fully integrated marketing agency based in Seattle, WA. What started as a media agency in 1977 is now an agency with full marketing capabilities. The comprehensive list of its services includes advertising, brand strategy, design, digital/Web, media and public relations.

GreenRubino serves top regional, national and international clients. Those clients include Delta Dental, Fred Hutchinson Cancer Research Center, Washington State Wine Commission, Snoqualmie Casino, Redhook Brewery and Fluke.

- 50 employees
- Annual revenue: $21M
- Percentage of revenue spent on leadership development: NA
- www.greenrubino.com

John Rubino, Partner

With more than 25 years of experience in branding, finance and operations, John provides a strategic expertise that combines knowledge of all aspects of both the business and design worlds. On GreenRubino client projects, John is the common thread uniting business goals with design solutions, acting as a strategic director in the process.

John established his reputation for strategic success during his ten-year stint with Landor Associates, a leading branding and design agency, where he led the global relationship with Microsoft and created an efficient, process-driven model that is now a benchmark for the way in which strategic design firms do business.

INTERNATIONAL COMMUNITY HEALTH SERVICES (ICHS), TERESITA BATAYOLA

International Community Health Services (ICHS) is a Federally qualified health center providing affordable health care to the uninsured and underinsured in the Asian Pacific Islander, immigrant, refugee and broader communities. ICHS annually serves people who speak more than 50 languages through full-service medical and dental clinics located in Seattle's International District and Holly Park neighborhoods; a school-based medical, behavioral health, and dental clinic at the Seattle World School; a full-service mobile dental coach serving 10 schools; and a primary care clinic at ACRS, a human services and mental health non-profit organization. ICHS is adding clinics in the cities of Bellevue and Shoreline.

- 300 employees serving more than 19,000 patients
- Annual revenue: $22 million
- Percentage of revenue spent on leadership development: $0; internal leadership training is incorporated in on-site training plans, but no funds are specifically allocated for leadership training.
- www.ichs.com

Teresita Batayola, CEO

As chief executive officer of International Community Health Services (ICHS) in Seattle, Washington, Teresita leads the state's largest Asian and Pacific Islander non-profit organization. ICHS provides primary healthcare services, including medical, dental, behavioral health, acupuncture and health education services. Teresita came to health care with a background in economic development, community and international development, and strategic planning.

Teresita is president of the Washington Association of Community and Migrant Health Centers and serves on the boards of the Association of Asian Pacific Community Health Organizations, the Community Health Plan, Community Health Network and the Community Clinic Contracting Network. Teresita is an active spokesperson and public speaker on affordable health care. In 2010, Teresita was named by *Seattle Business Magazine* as an outstanding leader in healthcare. In March, 2012, Teresita received the Betsey K. Cooke Grassroots MVP Award from the National Association of Community Health Centers. She holds a BA in Public Affairs from Seattle University and an MS in Urban Administration from Bucknell University.

JP MORGAN CHASE, PACIFIC NORTHWEST REGION, PHYLLIS CAMPBELL

JP Morgan Chase is a national financial services firm based in New York City. For the Pacific Northwest region:

- 4,200 employees (in Washington, Oregon and Idaho)
- $1.3 billion annual gross revenue for commercial banking business, real estate, asset management and retail
- Estimated percentage of revenue spent on leadership development: NA
- www.jpmorganchase.com

Phyllis Campbell, Chairman of the Pacific Northwest Region

Phyllis is the firm's most senior executive in the region and represents all lines of business to clients in the Pacific Northwest region of North America.

Previously, Phyllis was the president/CEO of The Seattle Foundation, the largest community foundation in Washington, with nearly $600 million in charitable assets. Earlier, she served as president and CEO of U.S. Bank of Washington. Phyllis holds an MBA from the University of Washington, and a BA in business administration from Washington State University. She holds honorary doctorates from Whitworth University and Gonzaga University.

She devotes her time, energy, and expertise to countless civic activities, with a focus on education and human services issues. Currently, she serves on the boards of Alaska Air Group, Nordstrom, PATH and Initiative for Global Development as well as the Diversity Advisory Board for Toyota, North America. Among the awards she has received are the Woman Who Makes a Difference Award from the International Women's Forum, the Top Women in Finance Award from Women of Color Magazine, and the 36th Regents' Distinguished Alumnus Award in 2006 from Washington State University.

MAVERON,
DAN LEVITAN

Maveron is a venture capital firm that invests exclusively in consumer companies and has raised approximately $900 million. The firm has offices in Seattle and San Francisco. Representative Maveron investments include eBay, zulily, General Assembly, Julep, Trupanion and Potbelly Sandwich Works.

- 15 employees
- Annual revenue: NA
- Percentage of revenue spent on leadership development: NA
- www.maveron.com

Dan Levitan, Co-Founder and Partner

Dan has 25 years of experience in venture capital and investing, specializing in leading consumer and retail businesses. Eager to help innovative companies realize their full potential, Dan launched Maveron in 1998, with Howard Schultz, chairman, president and chief executive officer of Starbucks Coffee Company. In this role, Dan has led many Maveron successful exits within the last 15 years, including, Capella Education Company (NASDAQ:CPLA), Cranium (acquired by Hasbro NASDAQ:HAS), Quellos (acquired by Blackrock NASDAQ:BLK), Good Technology (acquired by Motorola NASDAQ:MOT) and Shutterfly (NASDAQ:SFLY). He currently serves on the board of directors for PayNearMe, Pinkberry, Potbelly Sandwich Works (NASDAQ: PBPB), Trupanion and zulily (NASDAQ: ZU). Dan was named to the *Forbes* Midas List of Top Tech Investors in 2014. Dan is also a board member for The Rock Center for Entrepreneurship at Harvard Business School and the Seattle Children's Hospital Foundation. He graduated from Horace Mann School, and received a BA magna cum laude from Duke University and an MBA from Harvard Business School.

NBC KING 5,
RAY HEACOX

As the first television station in the Northwest, KING 5 delivers the largest local news audience and the most local programming. KING 5's content and programming lead the marketplace with three million monthly television viewers, and a combined 30 million monthly page views for KING 5 desktop, mobile and apps.

- Number of employees: NA
- Annual revenue: NA
- Percentage of revenue spent on leadership development: NA
- www.king5.com

Ray Heacox, President and General Manager

Ray is president and general manager of KING 5, KONG TV, NWCN (a regional cable and satellite news channel), King5.com and nwcn.com. All are part of Gannett Company, Inc., the nation's largest local media company.

While serving as president in Seattle, Ray also served for 18 months as the vice president of digital operations at Belo Corp., then-owner of KING 5. Prior to joining KING 5 in Seattle, Ray was the first director of the Paul F. Harron Graduate Program in Television Management at Drexel University in Philadelphia. He was in charge of creating a two-year, full-time, dual-degree (MS/MBA) curriculum. Simultaneously, he was the principal of Deft Management, providing consulting services to clients in media, technology and sales. During the 1990s, Ray held several prominent management positions with NBC, including president and general manager of KNBC in Los Angeles and EVP of sales for the NBC-owned and operated station group. Ray left NBC in 2000 to become president – and later CEO – of Media Ocean Inc., a business-to-business technology company.

Under his leadership, KING 5 has received three regional Emmy awards for overall station excellence. In addition, Ray has received several recent honors, including: the 2013 AJC Human Relations award for community service, 2012 *Broadcasting and Cable Magazine* GM of the year for large markets, the PLU Distinguished Alumnus Award for 2012, and the 2012 Greater NW MS Society Hope Award.

Ray grew up in Tacoma, Washington, and graduated from Pacific Lutheran University. Ray is trustee and chair of the ArtsFund Board, past chair of the National Multiple Sclerosis Society/Greater Northwest Chapter, a member of the Seattle Children's Hospital Foundation board, past member of the Benaroya Research Institute board of directors, past member of the American Heart Association Seattle, former board member of the Ricardo Montalban Nosotros Foundation, and a past member of the NBC Affiliates board. He lives in Seattle with his wife, Cynthia Huffman.

OKI GOLF AND OKI DEVELOPMENTS, INC., SCOTT OKI

Oki Golf is a collection of 11 premier Puget Sound golf courses providing championship golf course layouts and outstanding course conditions to players of all skill levels. With several Northwest golf courses located near Seattle, Everett and Olympia, Oki Golf's challenging course designs and unrivaled guest service provide an exceptional golf experience at unparalleled value to casual golfers, tournaments, and group outings.

- Number of employees: NA
- Annual revenue: NA
- Percentage of revenue spent on leadership development: NA
- www.okigolf.com

Scott Oki, Founder & Chairman

Scott is a professed entrepreneur, venture capitalist, philanthropist and community activist. His personal mission statement is "to marry my passion for things entrepreneurial with things philanthropic in ways that encourage others to do the same." Prior to founding Oki Developments, Inc., Scott retired after 10 years with Microsoft Corporation, where he founded the International Division and later served as senior vice president, sales, marketing and services.

Scott has served on more than 100 advisory boards and boards of directors for both for-profit and not-for-profit companies. He has founded or co-founded 20 non-profit organizations. In addition to his philanthropic activities through The Oki Foundation, he has taken leadership roles in many other organizations. He is the co-founder of Sounders For Kids, Seattle Parks Foundation, America's Foundation for Chess, First Tee of Greater Seattle, Social

Venture Partners, Microsoft Alumni Foundation, Seattle Police Foundation, and SeeYourImpact.org and is founder and chairman of TheParentsUnion.org. He has served as co-chair of the United Way of King County Campaign Board, Co-chair of the Million Dollar Roundtable, founder and chairman of the Japanese American Chamber of Commerce, founder of the Chief Seattle Council Boy Scout Scoutreach Foundation, and founder and chairman of Densho. He is a past-president of the board of regents for the University of Washington and former chair of the Children's Hospital Foundation. Scott has also served on the national boards for United Way of America, Boys & Girls Clubs of America, Japanese American National Museum, Boy Scouts of America and the U.S. Ski and Snowboard Team Foundation.

PROJECT BIONIC,
JOSH DIRKS

Project Bionic offers a myriad of services in the social media and mobile realm. First and foremost, the company is a team of curators of clients' social media presence. For its clients, the company serves as social media content creators, a social media analytics team, social media planners, social media strategists, social media community managers, ancillary marketing social media integrators, and social media auditors.

- 16 employees
- $1.3 million gross annual revenue
- Percentage of revenue spent on leadership development 9.2%
- www.projectbionic.com

Josh Dirks, CEO & Founder

Josh is an old hand at new media. He made his first big moves at Door-to-Door Moving and Storage, where his leadership and work ethic resulted in record earnings for his division and created an online marketing strategy that's still used today. Josh next joined the internet marketing world at 10X Marketing, a company founded by Paul Allen to provide full-service Web marketing services to businesses. He became a senior member of the team that launched 10X's proprietary SEO technology to an international market.

After 10X was acquired, Josh created Pin Point Marketing, which specialized in search engine optimization, pay-per-click and affiliate marketing. Not satisfied with one new company, he quickly became a founding member of three other high-tech ventures: AdBasix, Great American Scavenger Hunt and BlaghNow. Additionally, he also launched ExtremeNW, a social networking site for Northwest adventure seekers.

In 2007, Josh joined Entercom Communications as director of digital and strategic sales and marketing. In this role he became a thought leader in media integration and how to harness the power of social media within the traditional space. Many of the campaigns he worked on became the company's most successful.

Over the last three and half years, Josh and partners have been busy with Project Bionic, a company dedicated to humanizing brands beyond human capabilities. Today, Project Bionic has more than 50 clients and has grown month over month since its inception, continuing to break new ground and create proprietary solutions for the social and mobile media space.

During his spare time, Josh enjoys time with his wife, two small children and fox terrier. He is an avid sports fan, and loves networking with new people on a professional and personal level. Josh is proud to say he is a leading advocate of social media sites.

THE SEATTLE FOUNDATION, NORM RICE

Founded in 1946, The Seattle Foundation is the region's local, definitive resource for charitable giving. Whatever their charitable budget, The Seattle Foundation helps people give wisely so their philanthropy makes a difference and is personally rewarding.

One of the nation's largest community foundations, The Seattle Foundation has total assets of nearly 750 million. It is governed by a board of respected community leaders.

- Close to 40 employees
- Annual revenue: NA
- Percentage of revenue spent on leadership development: NA
- www.seattlefoundation.org

Norm Rice, President & CEO

Norm is leading the Seattle Foundation, one of the nation's largest community foundations, in achieving its mission to create a healthy community through engaged philanthropy, community knowledge and leadership.

Norm is former president and chief executive officer of the Federal Home Loan Bank of Seattle, a $48 billion bank. Retired in March 2005, he assumed his chief executive responsibilities in February 1999. In this post, he brought his passion and commitment for housing and community development to the private sector and worked with more than 375 financial institutions to make their communities better places to work and live.

Prior to his work at the Federal Home Loan Bank, Norm served two terms as mayor of Seattle from 1990 to 1997. In this role, he earned national acclaim for revitalizing Seattle's downtown and strengthening the city neighborhoods through public-private partnerships. While in office, he championed for an improved public school system, breathed new life into Seattle's downtown with new retail centers, housing and civic buildings, and implemented a welfare-to-work program.

Norm is the recipient of numerous professional and community awards, including the American Jewish Committee's Human Relations Award (presented to both Mr. Rice and his wife, Dr. Constance Rice), the National Award for Leadership on Behalf of Neighborhoods from the National Neighborhood Coalition, the Isabel Coleman Pierce Award from the King County Chapter of the YWCA, the Mark F. Cooper Leadership Award from the Washington Council on Crime and Delinquency, and the American Association of Community College Students' Outstanding Alumni Award.

Currently, Norm is a member of the White House Council for Community Solutions and the Brookings Institution's Advisory Committee for Sustainable Communities. He serves as chairman of the board of directors for the Northwest African-American Museum and is past chair of the Enterprise Foundation, Fifth Avenue Theatre, YMCA of Greater Seattle and United Way of King County. He also serves on the boards of the King County Committee to End Homelessness and HistoryLink. Norm holds a bachelor of arts degree in communications and a master of arts degree in public administration from the University of Washington. He holds honorary doctorates from Cornish College of the Arts, Seattle University, University of Puget Sound and Whitman College.

METROPOLITAN SEATTLE CHAMBER OF COMMERCE, MAUD DAUDON

The Seattle Metropolitan Chamber of Commerce is the largest and most diverse business association in the Puget Sound region. Founded in 1882 by local business leaders, the Chamber today is an independent organization representing 2,200 companies and a regional workforce of approximately 700,000.

- 70-80 employees, including six affiliate locations.
- Non-profit, $5-8 million annual revenue
- Percentage of revenue spent on leadership development: NA
- www.seattlechamber.com

Maud Daudon, CEO

Maud was appointed Chamber president and CEO on June 19, 2012. She stepped into this role after 10 years with Seattle-Northwest Securities Corporation (SNW), a Seattle-based independent, employee-owned, regionally focused investment bank, broker-dealer and asset management firm specializing in debt securities and related businesses. For the latter six years she served as president and CEO of the firm. In this capacity, Maud navigated the toughest period in financial services since the Great Depression. She restored the profitability of the firm and maintained the firm's independent, locally focused leadership.

From 1998 to 2001, Maud was deputy mayor and chief of staff for the city of Seattle, focusing on overall city strategy, public safety, labor issues, budget, information technology, and city utilities. Before that, Maud was the chief financial officer for the Port of Seattle for six years and held other finance-related positions at the port for the previous two years. She gained significant experience in public finance by working for six years completing transportation and public works-related bond financings for a national investment banking firm in its New York and Seattle offices.

Maud is currently the chair of the Washington Student Achievement Council, co-chair of WSDOT and the city of Seattle's Advisory Committee on Tolling and Traffic, chairs the board of trustees for the Bullitt Foundation, and serves on the board of trustees for Seattle Biomedical Research Institute. She was recently named as a member of Governor-elect Jay Inslee's transition team. Past leadership roles include serving on Governor Gregoire's Higher Education Funding Task Force. In 2010, she was recognized as one of the *Puget Sound Business Journal's* Women of Influence.

Maud has been active with the Chamber for more than 20 years. From September 2010 to September 2011, she served a one-year term as volunteer chair of the Chamber, where she helped to establish the Chamber's comprehensive plan.

Maud has a master of public and private management (M.P.P.M.) with emphasis on finance and economic development from the Yale School of Organization and Management and a B.A. from Hampshire College. She and her husband, Marc, have two children and live in the Madrona neighborhood in Seattle.

SEATTLE UNIVERSITY, FATHER STEPHEN SUNDBORG

Seattle University, founded in 1891, is a Jesuit Catholic university and law school located on 50 acres in Seattle's Capitol Hill neighborhood. More than 7,400 students are enrolled in undergraduate and graduate programs within eight schools and colleges.

The university ranks number six among 121 regional universities in the West that provide a full range of undergraduate and master's degree programs, according to *U.S. News & World Report: Best Colleges 2014.*

- 1,400 employees
- Annual revenue: NA
- Percentage of revenue spent on leadership development: NA
- www.seattleu.edu

Father Stephen Sundborg, President

Father Stephen Sundborg became president of Seattle University in July, 1997. He leads a comprehensive, independent university of more than 7,400 undergraduate and graduate students and 1,400 faculty and staff members.

Since becoming president, Father Sundborg's key objectives have been to encourage student-centered education, enhance academic excellence, and develop resources to support a growing student population. During his tenure, Seattle University has built a new law school, a student center, student residences, a library and sports facilities. Father Sundborg is strongly committed to promoting social justice, a core value of the Jesuit Catholic education. As President, Father Sundborg has bestowed honorary degrees on such social justice leaders as Nelson Mandela, Archbishop Desmond Tutu, and Corazon Aquino.

Father Sundborg grew up in the Territory of Alaska. He entered the Jesuits in 1961 and was ordained a priest in Seattle in 1974. He completed his doctoral studies in spirituality at the Pontifical Gregorian University in Rome in 1982. He taught theology at Seattle University from 1982-1990, was appointed Rector of the Seattle University Jesuit community in 1986, and served as provincial of the Northwest Jesuits from 1990 to 1996. Father Sundborg is the twenty-first president to lead Seattle University since it was founded in 1891.

SPECIAL OLYMPICS WASHINGTON, BETH WOJICK

Special Olympics Washington provides year-round sports training and athletic competition in a variety of Olympic-type sports for children and adults with intellectual disabilities, giving them continuing opportunities to develop physical fitness, demonstrate courage, experience joy and participate in the sharing of gifts, skills and friendship with their families, other Special Olympics athletes and the community.

- 29 employees; more than 8,000 volunteers
- Annual revenue: $5 million
- Percentage of revenue spent on leadership development: .05%
- www.specialolympicswashington.org

Beth Wojick, CEO

Beth is president and CEO of Special Olympics Washington and has held this position since 2008. The statewide organization coordinates and produces more than 140 sports and programs each year for 10,000 athletes with and without intellectual disabilities. Beth is credited with starting the first-ever public schools Special Olympics program in Washington State. In addition to her local responsibilities, Beth is the chair of the SONA Special Olympics Disaster Relief Committee and served on the United States Leadership Council, chaired the SONA Technology Committee, participated in the Eunice K. Shriver Fellowship program, and participated in the Special Olympics International strategic planning meeting held in Morocco.

Beth began her career in 1986 at Seafair, a non-profit special events organization that produces more than 40 events each summer. Starting in event production, she was eventually promoted to associate managing director. In 1993, Beth was recruited by the Seattle Mariners to be director of corporate marketing, leading the organizations' corporate, suite and ticket sales campaigns. In 1997, the Seafair board of directors recruited Beth to come back as the new CEO and she is credited with saving the festival and creating its first Seafair Marathon (now the Rock n' Roll Marathon). In 2005, Beth was recruited by the Seattle Seahawks to be vice president of corporate partnerships, where she was responsible for sponsorships, broadcast rights, suites and major special events. Before joining Special Olympics, Beth was the executive director of business development for One Reel, a non-profit festival organization and producers of Bumbershoot and Teatro ZinZanni.

Beth was named one of the Newsmaker's of the Year by the *Puget Sound Business Journal*, she was a finalist for the Sports Commission's MVP of the Year award, and she received a Lifetime Achievement award from the King County Event Producers Association.

Beth currently serves on the board of directors of the Seattle Sports Commission and the Washington Athletic Club. After the 9-11 attacks, Beth was a founding co-chair of the Seattle Police Foundation and served on its board of directors for more than 10 years.

A Colorado native, Beth graduated from the University of Colorado with a degree in commercial recreation. She is married to John Wojick, a senior executive with The Boeing Company.

STE. MICHELLE WINE ESTATES, TED BASELER

Ste. Michelle Wine Estates, the third-largest producer of premium wine in the U.S., is a collection of distinctive wine estates. The Ste. Michelle Wine Estates company provides administrative and financial support for these wine properties, which include:

- *Washington State*: Chateau Ste. Michelle, Columbia Crest, Northstar, Col Solare, Spring Valley Vineyard, 14 Hands
- *Oregon*: Erath
- *California*: Stag's Leap Wine Cellars, Conn Creek

Ste. Michelle Wine Estates is also the exclusive U.S. importer for Antinori wines of Italy, Champagne Nicholas Feuillatte of France, and Villa Maria Estate in New Zealand.

- 1,050 employees
- Annual Revenue: $561 million in 2012
- Estimated percentage of revenue spent on leadership development: <1%
- www.ste-michelle.com

Ted Baseler, President & CEO

Ted joined the company in 1984 after working on the Chateau Ste. Michelle account as a vice president for Cole & Weber in Seattle. Over the years, Ted has risen through the ranks and became president and CEO in 2001. Since then, Ted has turned around company profit growth by increasing quality, focusing on Washington vineyards, acquiring highly acclaimed small wineries, and expanding distribution worldwide. The company has had record earnings in 11 of the 12 years since Ted took the helm. His leadership roles in the industry have included chairman of the Washington Wine Commission, chairman of the Wine Market Council, and director of the Washington Wine Institute. *Wine Enthusiast* magazine named Ted Man of the Year in 2009. He also led efforts to create an enology and viticulture program at Washington State University, where he has served on the board of regents. Ted's previous employment includes working as an account executive for J. Walter Thompson in Chicago, where his emphasis was on packaged goods marketing. Ted received a bachelor's degree from Washington State University and a master's degree from Northwestern University.

TOM DOUGLAS RESTAURANTS, PAMELA HINCKLEY

Tom Douglas, along with partners Jackie Cross and Eric Tanaka, is the chef-owner of numerous Seattle restaurants and businesses. Tom Douglas Restaurants includes: Dahlia Lounge, Etta's, Seatown, Rub with Love Shack, Palace Kitchen, Lola, Serious Pie Virginia, Serious Pie Westlake, Serious Biscuit, Dahlia Bakery, Cuoco, Brave Horse Tavern, TanakaSan, Assembly Hall Juice and Coffee, and Home Remedy. The opening of Home Remedy, an urban grocery and deli including a salad bar and a made-to-order menu, marks a full-fledged foray into creating the company's own line of frozen and refrigerated prepared foods. The company also runs professional bread and pastry bakeries called the Dahlia Workshop, a catering business called Tom Douglas' Catering and Events, and an event space called the Palace Ballroom, as well as operating the concessions at the Paramount and Moore theaters.

- 750 - 800 employees
- Annual revenue: $45 million
- Percentage of revenue spent on leadership development: 1% spent on leadership development in the form of weekly meetings, internal training and guest speakers.
- www.tomdouglas.com

Pamela Hinckley, CEO

After graduating with a degree in psychology from Suffolk University in the mid 1970s, Pamela went to work in her field in a private psychiatric hospital and quickly became disheartened by psychology in practice. Raised with a strong sense of community service, she signed up for a two-year stint with Vista (now Americorps). Her task was to create a farmers market, and she was drawn into the world of food and beverage. Years in multiple levels of the wine business followed, and then she became vice president of marketing for Redhook Brewery. She followed that with two years of marketing consulting. One client was Theo Chocolate, a company she invested in and helped launch. Four years ago, Tom Douglas asked Pamela to join his team as CEO.

UNIVERSITY OF WASHINGTON MEDICINE, DR. PAUL RAMSEY

UW Medicine owns or operates Harborview Medical Center, Northwest Hospital & Medical Center, Valley Medical Center, University of Washington Medical Center, a network of nine UW Neighborhood Clinics that provide primary care and secondary care, a physician practice plan UW Physicians, the UW School of Medicine and Airlift Northwest. In addition, UW Medicine shares in the ownership and governance of Children's University Medical Group and Seattle Cancer Care Alliance, a partnership among UW Medicine, Fred Hutchinson Cancer Research Center and Seattle Children's.

- More than 24,000 employees.
- Annual revenue: $4 billion
- Percentage of revenue spent on leadership development: NA
- www.uwmedicine.org

Dr. Paul G. Ramsey, CEO and Dean of the School of Medicine

Paul is the CEO of UW Medicine, executive vice president for medical affairs and dean of the School of Medicine at the University of Washington. He has served as the senior executive leader of UW Medicine since June, 1997.

Paul graduated from Harvard College in 1971 with honors in bio-chemistry and received his M.D. from Harvard Medical School in 1975. Following completion of residency training in internal med-icine at Massachusetts General Hospital, he came to the University of Washington in 1978. He served as acting chair and then chair of the UW Department of Medicine from 1990 to 1997, when he was appointed to his current administrative leadership position. Paul was the first holder of the Robert G. Petersdorf Endowed Chair in Medicine in 1995. He has received the Distinguished Teacher Award from the University of Washington School of Medicine's graduating class three times (in 1984, 1986, and 1987) and the Margaret Anderson Award from the University of Washington graduating class of 1989; the award recognizes exceptional support of medical students.

Paul's research has focused on the development of methods to assess physicians' clinical competence. He has been the principal investigator on multiple research grants related to assessment of physicians' clinical skills and served as a Henry J. Kaiser Family Foundation Faculty Scholar in general internal medicine for five years. Paul received the John P. Hubbard Award from the National Board of Medical Examiners in 1999 in recognition of his research contributions in the field of evaluation. He has served on many national committees and is a member of multiple organizations, including serving as an elected member of the Association of American Physicians and the Institute of Medicine of the National Academy of Sciences.

XTREME CONSULTING, GREG RANKICH

Xtreme Consulting's mission is to inspire, enable and empower its employees, its clients and its communities to prosper. Its business and technology professionals are focused on improving business performance for clients of all types and sizes. Xtreme Teams™ catalyze innovation, inspiring and delivering superior results.

- Nearly 800 employees
- Annual revenue: $80 million
- Percentage of revenue spent on leadership development: No cap
- www.xtremeconsulting.com

Greg Rankich, CEO

Greg has led Xtreme from its inception in 2005, managing the overall corporate strategic planning and operations as well as personnel and financial functions. He oversees corporate marketing strategies, employee programs, community relationships, and internal and external communication.

Prior to founding Xtreme, Greg held many roles within Microsoft, including worldwide management of Microsoft high performance computing efforts. Greg also helped manage enterprise deployments between Microsoft and Compaq, managed the product launch of Windows Server 2000 Datacenter Server, and played a key role in the competitive landscape of Microsoft in the enterprise space.

Greg was an honoree in the 2008 *Puget Sound Business Journal* "40 under 40" awards. In 2010, Greg was a finalist for the Ernst & Young Entrepreneur of the Year award. Greg is an active Washington State University Foundation trustee, member of the CEO Project organization and the American Staffing Association, and is involved in numerous charities and nonprofits in the Northwest. When not working, Greg is usually spending time with his wife and two kids, relaxing on a golf course, boating around Lake Washington, or playing poker. Greg holds a B.A. and an M.B.A. from Washington State University.

MORE QUESTIONS, SOME ANSWERS AND A FINAL NOTE

In business, two key questions I ask myself and others are: "How do you deliver impact?" and "How do you measure the result?"

My answers are usually variations of:

Because I am impatient, have a clear sense of urgency and a high get-it factor, I read people quickly, identify their strengths and help them develop strategies to move themselves forward.

My performance is defined by the results I get for the people I work with.

So, how did this book deliver impact for you and how do *you* measure the result?

The bottom line is, we need more great leaders. We have a shortage and we need to change that.

For some, being a leader is about driving individual results, receiving accolades and recognition and basking in their own greatness. I didn't interview them.

The leaders in this book are the leaders who get it. Simply stated, they model great leadership and look for ways to develop others. They actively listen, show compassion and empathy, keep a sense of humor and hold humility at their core. They have a greater sense of purpose, which is to develop others.

Those are the leaders we need to replicate – more leaders like you, who are active and deliberate in growing yourself in order to develop others. To have a hand in helping someone else build his or her greatness is the impact by which we can and *should* be measured.

And that's the performance measure I challenge you to employ as you explore your answers to the questions posed throughout the book.

EXPLORE ANSWERS. What! You didn't answer them as you were reading? Well, grab a pen! They're listed in full below. (Or, better yet, go to www.FromTheCEOsPerspective.com and download them.)

TAKE ACTION. After you've answered them, the next step is ACTION. Write out the 10 actions you're going to take over the next 90 days to further develop your own leadership and to help develop someone else's.

CALL ME. Here's my relatively private cell number 206.719.5001. I can't wait to hear your plan, brainstorm more ideas or discuss the one thing you think could help you be a more impactful leader. And if we run out of things to talk about, we can always resort to my next favorite subject: wine.

Good luck!

Jeri Cotterman

IN YOUR OWN WORDS

YOUR STORY, YOUR PASSION

1. Who had a key impact on *you* as a leader? Why?

2. Of all the famous leaders you know or have read about, with whom do you most identify and why?

3. Which of the leaders' answers most surprise you?

4. Have you served as mentor to a future leader? If so, what do you think were the most important things you imparted?

5. If you haven't yet been a mentor, could you be? What are the most significant lessons you would like to instill?

GENERATIONAL ANGST

6. Which of the stereotypes about your generation are true of you? (Be honest)

7. What bugs you most about other generations? How can you resolve those differences or change those perceptions?

8. What have you or can you learn from other generations?

9. As a leader, what can you do to bring different generations together?

10. How might generational differences affect the future of your organization? What can you do now to build a stronger future?

DEFINING LEADERSHIP

11. Which one or two core values define who you are?

12. How do you express and reinforce those values at work? (In other words, how do people know what your values are? If they don't know, why not?)

13. How are your values integrated into the organization? (Consider how the organization recruits and hires, what the organization rewards, and so on.)

14. How do you ensure employees drive decisions based on those values?

15. What do you need to stop doing to ensure you're living your values?

IDENTIFYING FUTURE LEADERS

16. Do you have a list of high-potential people in your head?

17. What qualities do you look for? How do you assess for those qualities?

18. What experiences, mistakes and failures were most helpful to you in developing your own leadership skills?

19. What are you doing, formally and informally, to help develop the high-potential people in your organization?

20. Is your leadership development process consistent with the organization's values? If so, how? If not, what do you need to do to make it so?

TAKING YOUR OWN ADVICE

21. On a scale of 1-10, how self-aware do you think you are as a leader? What do you think is your best leadership strength? Why?

22. What one quality do you think every leader must have? How do you assess for that quality when hiring or promoting others?

23. Did the must-have qualities named by the leaders impact your thinking in any way? If so, how?

24. Which qualities or behaviors have you seen most often derail leaders? Do you see that behavior in yourself? What do you think you need to stop doing to be a better leader?

25. How has technology challenged you as a leader? What do you need to do to manage decreasing time and increasing technology?

ABOUT THE AUTHOR

Teri Citterman is a student of the question. She has a fearless curiosity and finds that the best way to get to know someone is by inquiring…

As an author, speaker, certified executive coach, writing coach and ghostwriter, what is your mission?

My mission is to be a mind reader: To help leaders articulate their messages, by conveying what they're truly thinking, in a way that engages and motivates employees, customers, investors and other stakeholders.

What is your edge?

I have a keen ear for what's not being said — and can quickly connect insights to actions that move people forward.

You say you're fearlessly curious. What does that mean?

I'm fearless in my approach. I pose the challenging questions others think, but don't ask. Those are what open the doors to the powerful thinking. It's the same approach I take with my passion for trapeze. I listen with laser focus, jump in with no fear and wait for the weightless moments – where the boldest insights reveal themselves.

What do you consider your super power?

Courage.

How'd you get to this point?

My experience draws on 20 years of advising CEOs on issues related to internal and external communications. Formerly, I served as head of corporate communications for a leading education technology company. In addition, I'm an award-winning wine writer, author of *Best Places to Kiss in the Northwest*, and contributor to the *Puget Sound* and *Portland Business Journal*s, *Wine Press Northwest* and *Seattle Metropolitan Magazine* on entrepreneurship, biotech, technology, education, retail, real estate, hospitality and lifestyle.

What are people surprised to find out about you?

I have EU citizenship.

What are your favorite things?

Travel, wine, aerial trapeze, skiing and watching movies early in the morning while it's still dark out. I'm part of a child-raising-team for a fantastic 11 year old. I think I'm very lucky.

COACHING

What's your edge?

Every leader in this book has a clearly defined edge. They demonstrate it, they speak it, they live it. It's an amalgamation of their values and the self-recognition they have of their unique strengths. It's what makes them strong, effective and interesting leaders.

What is it that sets you apart from all the other charismatic generics out there holding the company reigns? You may be smarter. You may be better suited. But they know their edge. They communicate it and demonstrate it, and that leads to success.

Executives hire me when they're looking to sharpen their edge, when they want to drive their career to the next level. Similarly, up-and-coming high performers work with me to out-position the rest of the smart-aggressives and propel their career forward toward those coveted executive roles.

The endgame is a sharpened awareness of your unique strengths (not the ones you think you have, but the ones that actually set you apart from the working population), how you use them and how they impact others.

I'm happy to spend 30 minutes talking with you to see if this might be a valuable process for you. Send me a note: Teri@Talonnllc.com. For more information www.Tallonnllc.com.

GHOSTWRITING & BOOK COACHING

Hemingway said: *There is nothing to writing.*
All you have to do is sit down at a typewriter and bleed.

He wasn't kidding.

Having a book is a game changer. It's an impressive show of courage, credibility and commitment. It opens doors and uncovers possibilities that springboard you into new opportunities and new relationships. That springboard becomes a trampoline of visibility, leading to lucrative speaking engagements, more media coverage and ultimately more business.

But it's not for the faint of heart.

You have to want it. You have to get your helmet on and get in the game every day. Writing is a psychological exercise in discipline, endurance and despair.

The writing process is not for everyone. And to be clear, neither am I.

Fortunately, some people still want to go down the path and they choose to go down it with me. Business leaders hire me to extract their experiences and craft them into compelling stories. I help them convey their knowledge, direct their message or develop the platform from which they want to leap (sometimes).

Some of them are skilled writers; some are not. The equalizer is that few of them have the time, inclination or know-how to start *and finish* the book that everyone's been telling them to write.

You can go at it alone. You can hire a coach. Or you can hire a ghost. I'm happy to spend 30 minutes brainstorming to see which one of those ways is the best one for you. Give me a call at 206.719.5001 (yes, I'll pick up) or contact me via email at Teri@Talonnllc.com. For more information, www.Talonnllc.com.

Cheers!

SPEAKING

Teri engages with the audience and speaks passionately on a variety of topics related to leadership, communication and influence. Some of the most requested topics include:

Generational Leadership Bubbling in the Cauldron

- For the first time in history, we have four, nearly five generations working in our organizations. And like it or not, we are products of our generations. When it comes to talking movies, that can be either baffling or amusing. But when it comes to working together, it can be irritating, frustrating or infuriating.

Powerbase and Influence

- Assessing the power in your network and developing a simple influence strategy to know the right people for the right reasons.

Who Do You Think You Are?

- The Power of Perception and how it stops you from achieving your potential.

Be a Bad-Ass Author

- Translate the idea out of your head and into *the* book

To book Teri for speaking at your next event, contact:

info@Talonnllc.com
206.719.5001
www.Talonnllc.com
www.FromTheCeosPerspective.com

#CEOpov

ALSO BY TERI CITTERMAN

The Best Places to Kiss in the Northwest, 10th Ed.,
published by Sasquatch Books

The Northwest Wine Journal,
published by Sasquatch Books

ENDNOTES

PART 3: BREAKING IT DOWN

1. Jeff Schwartz, Josh Bersin and Bill Pelster, *Global Human Capital Trends 2014: Engaging the 21st-Century Workforce*, Deloitte University Press, 2014. www.deloitte.com

2. Kim Morgan, "*Fight Club* Ten Years Later," *The Huffington Post*, November 19, 2009.

3. "*The Social Network* and 12 More Movies That Defined a Generation," *Rolling Stone*, wwww.rollingstone.com, September 30, 2010.

4. "Generations in the Workplace in the United States and Canada," Catalyst, May 1, 2012. www.catalyst.org/knowledge

5. "Generations in the Workplace in the United States and Canada," Catalyst, May 1, 2012. www.catalyst.org/knowledge

6. "Generations in the Workplace in the United States and Canada," Catalyst, May 1, 2012. www.catalyst.org/knowledge

7. "Generations in the Workplace in the United States and Canada," Catalyst, May 1, 2012. www.catalyst.org/knowledge

8. "Country Note: United States," *Programme for International Student Assessment (PISA) 2012*, Organisation for Economic Co-operation and Development (OECD), Paris, 2012.

9. "College Preparedness Lacking, Forcing Students Into Developmental Coursework, Prompting Some to Drop Out," *The Huffington Post*, June 18, 2012.

10. Gloria Larson and Mike Metzger, "Why Everyone Is Wrong About Working With Millennials," *Fast Company*, December 3, 2013, www.fastcompany.com.

11. Jean M. Twenge and W. Keith Campbell, "Age and Birth Cohort Differences in Self-Esteem: A Cross-Temporal Meta- Analysis," *Personality and Social Psychology Review*, November 2001.

12. Jean M. Twenge, Sara Konrath, Joshua D. Foster, W. Keith Campbell and Brad J. Bushman, "Egos Inflating Over Time: A Cross-Temporal Meta-Analysis of the Narcissistic Personality Inventory," *Journal of Personality*, August 2008.

13. Jean M. Twenge, "A Review of the Empirical Evidence on Generational Differences in Work Attitudes," *Journal of Business and Psychology*, June 2010.

PART 4: DEFINING LEADERSHIP

1.   Jeff Schwartz, Josh Bersin and Bill Pelster, *Global Human Capital Trends 2014: Engaging the 21st-Century Workforce*, Deloitte University Press, 2014. www.deloitte.com

2.   Jim Kouzes and Barry Posner, *The Five Practices of Exemplary Leadership® Model*, www.leadershipchallenge.com. Also, Jim Kouzes and Barry Posner, *The Leadership Challenge: How To Make Extraordinary Things Happen in Organizations (Fifth Edition)*, Jossey-Bass, 2012.

PART 5: IDENTIFYING FUTURE LEADERS

1.   Jeff Schwartz, Josh Bersin and Bill Pelster, *Global Human Capital Trends 2014: Engaging the 21st-Century Workforce*, Deloitte University Press, 2014. www.deloitte.com

2.   Deloitte and *Forbes* Insights, "Talent Edge 2020: Blueprints for the New Normal," Deloitte, December 2010. www.deloitte.com

3.   Deloitte and *Forbes* Insights, "Talent Edge 2020: Blueprints for the New Normal," Deloitte, December 2010. www.deloitte.com

4.   Jeff Schwartz, Josh Bersin and Bill Pelster, *Global Human Capital Trends 2014: Engaging the 21st-Century Workforce*, Deloitte University Press, 2014. www.deloitte.com

5.   Deloitte and *Forbes* Insights, "Talent Edge 2020: Blueprints for the New Normal," Deloitte, December 2010. www.deloitte.com

6.   Jeff Schwartz, Josh Bersin and Bill Pelster, *Global Human Capital Trends 2014: Engaging the 21st-Century Workforce*, Deloitte University Press, 2014. www.deloitte.com

7.   Jeff Schwartz, Josh Bersin and Bill Pelster, *Global Human Capital Trends 2014: Engaging the 21st-Century Workforce*, Deloitte University Press, 2014. www.deloitte.com

8.   Jeff Schwartz, Josh Bersin and Bill Pelster, *Global Human Capital Trends 2014: Engaging the 21st-Century Workforce*, Deloitte University Press, 2014. www.deloitte.com

INDEX

"Whatever you can do, or dream you can do, begin it. Boldness has genius, power and magic in it."

—Johann Wolfgang von Goethe, 1749-1832

29917786R00130

Made in the USA
San Bernardino, CA
01 February 2016